ISBN 978-1-4400-8283-2
PIBN 10007496

This book is a reproduction of an important historical work. Forgotten Books uses
state-of-the-art technology to digitally reconstruct the work, preserving the original format
whilst repairing imperfections present in the aged copy. In rare cases, an imperfection in
the original, such as a blemish or missing page, may be replicated in our edition. We do,
however, repair the vast majority of imperfections successfully; any imperfections that
remain are intentionally left to preserve the state of such historical works.

1 MONTH OF FREE READING

at

www.ForgottenBooks.com

By purchasing this book you are eligible for one month membership to ForgottenBooks.com, giving you unlimited access to our entire collection of over 700,000 titles via our web site and mobile apps.

To claim your free month visit:

www.forgottenbooks.com/free7496

Similar Books Are Available from
www.forgottenbooks.com

CONTENTS

2210306

Preface to the Revised Edition

THIS revised edition of my Grammar of the Auxiliary International Language, "Esperanto" —the first published for English readers—has had the great advantage of the personal supervision and official approval of the founder, Dr. Zamenhof.

That it has been prepared to supply a want is not a mere *façon de parler*. Prior to the appearance of the first edition hundreds of inquirers, from most widely separated sections at home and abroad had written urgently requesting a grammar suitable for English students. These inquirers, for the most part, came to know of the existence of "Esperanto" through the medium of pamphlets, leaflets, letters in the public Press, etc., which could give, of necessity, only the merest idea and outline of the language.

In compiling a book to meet this demand my chief desire and aim has been to prepare a Grammar, which, while being complete in all its parts and containing everything that is necessary for a sound knowledge of the language, should be brief, clear, full, but not redundant.

To the following gentlemen I return my best thanks for their exceeding great kindness and cordial co-operation :—Monsieur L. de Beaufront, President of the Committee of Direction (for Esperanto) in France, who has written the "Conversations,"[1] etc., in Section II. ; The Honourable R. H. Geoghegan, to whom, in great measure, I am indebted for the chapter on the Participle ; Mr. Joseph Rhodes, F.J.S., President of the Esperanto Society, Keighley, Yorks (the first society established for the study of the language in England), who, despite his many literary duties, has given me valuable assistance in revising this new edition ; to Monsieur P. Ahlberg, President of the Esperanto Society, Stockholm, to whom I am indebted for the greater number of the Commercial letters in Section III. ; and to Mr. Charles Hayes, Wandsworth, who also has given me valuable assistance in preparing this Grammar for publication.

J. C. O'CONNOR, M.A.

17, St. Stephen's Square, Bayswater, W.

---

[1] These dialogues originally appeared in *L'Espérantiste* from the pen of Monsieur de Beaufront. This is a monthly journal, printed in French and Esperanto, and published in Paris. To all desirous of perfecting themselves in the language it will prove a most valuable aid. It can be had by applying to the Secretary, Esperanto Society, 10, Place de la Bourse, Paris.

THE MAKING OF AN INTERNATIONAL LANGUAGE.

[BY DR. ZAMENHOF.]

*From the "*FUNDAMENTA KRESTOMATIO,*" which every Esperantist should read.*

If the reader should take up this little work with an incredulous smile, supposing that he is about to peruse the impracticable schemes of some good citizen of Utopia, I would in the first place beg of him to lay aside all prejudice, and treat seriously and critically the question brought before him.

I need not here point out the considerable importance to humanity of an international language—a language unconditionally accepted by everyone, and the common property of the whole world. How much time and labour we spend in learning foreign tongues, and yet when travelling in foreign countries we are, as a rule, unable to converse with other human beings in their own language. How much time, labour, and money are wasted in translating the literary productions of one nation into the language of another, and yet, if we rely on translations alone, we can become acquainted with but a tithe of foreign literature.,

Were there but an international language all translations would be made into it alone, as into a tongue intelligible to all, and works of an international character would be written in it in the first instance. The Chinese wall dividing literatures would disappear, and the works of other nations would be as readily intelligible to us as those of our own authors. Books being the same for everyone, education, ideals, convictions, aims, would be the same too, and all nations would be united in a common brotherhood. Being compelled, as we now are, to devote our time to the study of several different languages, we cannot study any of them sufficiently well, and there are but few persons who can even boast a complete mastery of their mother-tongue. .On the other hand, language cannot progress towards perfection, and we are often obliged, even in speaking our own language, to borrow words and expressions from foreigners, or to express our thoughts inexactly.

How different would the case be had we but two languages to learn ; we should know them infinitely better, and the languages themselves would grow richer, and reach a higher degree of perfection than is found in any of those now existing. And yet though language is the prime motor of civilisation, and to it alone we owe the fact that we have raised ourselves above the level of other animals, difference of speech is a cause of antipathy, nay even of hatred, between people, as being the first thing to strike us on meeting. Not being understood we keep aloof, and the first notion that occurs to our minds is, not to find out whether the others are of our own political opinions, or whence their ancestors came from thousands of years ago, but to dislike the strange sound of their language. Moreover, anyone who has lived for a length of time in a commercial city, whose inhabitants were of different unfriendly nations, will easily understand what a boon would be conferred on mankind by the adoption of an international idiom, which, without interfering with domestic affairs or the private life of nations, would play the part of an official and commercial dialect, at any rate, in countries inhabited by people of different nationalities.

I will not expatiate on the immense importance which, it may well be imagined, an international language would acquire in science, commerce, etc. Whoever has but once bestowed a thought on the subject will surely acknowledge that no sacrifice would be too great if by it we could obtain a universal tongue. It is, therefore, imperative that the slightest effort in that direction should be attended to. The best years of my life have been devoted to this momentous cause.

I shall not here enter upon an analysis of the various attempts already made to give the public a universal language, but will content myself with remarking that these efforts have amounted either to a short system of mutually-intelligible signs, or to a natural simplification of the grammar of existing modern languages, with a change of their words into others arbitrarily formed. The attempts of the first category were quickly seen to be too complicated for practical use, and so faded into oblivion; those of the second were, perhaps, entitled to the name of "languages," but certainly not "international" languages. The inventors called their tongues "universal," I know not why, possibly because no one in the whole world, except themselves, could understand a single word written or spoken in any of them. If a language, in order to become universal, has but to be named so, then, forsooth, the wish of any single individual can frame out of any existing dialect a universal tongue. As these authors naively imagined that their essays would be enthusiastically welcomed and taken up by the whole world, and as this unanimous welcome is precisely what the cold and indifferent world declines to give, when there is no chance of realising any immediate benefit, it is not much to be marvelled at if these brilliant attempts came to nothing. The greater part of the world was not in the slightest degree interested in the prospect of a new language, and the persons who really cared about the matter thought it scarcely worth while to learn a tongue which none but the inventor could understand. When the whole world, said they, has learnt this language, or at least several million people, we will do the same.

I have always been interested in the question of a universal language, but as I did not feel myself better qualified for the work than the authors of so many other fruitless attempts, I did not risk running into print, and merely occupied myself with imaginary schemes and a minute study of the problem. At length, however, some happy ideas, the fruits of my reflections, incited me to further work, and induced me to essay the systematic conquest of the many obstacles which beset the path of the inventor of a new rational universal language. As it appears to me that I have almost succeeded in my undertaking, I am now venturing to lay before a critical public the results of my long and assiduous labours.

The principal difficulties to be overcome were :—

(1). To render the study of the language so easy as to make its acquisition mere play to the learner.

(2). To enable the learner to make direct use of his knowledge with persons of any nationality, whether the language be universally accepted or not ; in other words, the language is to be directly a means of international communication.

(3). To find some means of overcoming the natural indifference of mankind, and disposing them, in the quickest manner possible, and *en masse*, to learn and use the proposed language as a living one, and not only in last extremities, and with the key at hand.

Amongst the numberless projects submitted at various times to the public, often under the high-sounding but unaccountable name of "universal languages," no one has solved at once more than one of the above-mentioned problems, and even that but partially.

Before proceeding to enlighten the reader as to the

means employed for the solution of the problems, I would ask of him to reconsider the exact significance of each separately, so that he may not be inclined to quibble at my methods of solution merely because they may appear to him perhaps too simple. I do this because I am well aware that the majority of mankind feel disposed to bestow their consideration on any subject the more carefully, in proportion, as it is enigmatical and incomprehensible. Such persons, at the sight of so short a grammar, with rules so simple and so readily intelligible, will be ready to regard it with a contemptuous glance, never considering the fact—of which a little further reflection would convince them—that this simplification and bringing of each detail out of its original complicated form into the simplest and easiest conceivable was, in fact, the most insuperable obstacle to be overcome.

The First Difficulty.

The first of the problems was solved in the following manner :—

(1). I simplified the grammar to the utmost, and while, on the one hand, I carried out my object in the spirit of the existing modern languages, in order to make the study as free from difficulties as possible, on the other hand, I did not deprive it of clearness, exactness, and flexibility. My whole grammar can be learned perfectly in *one hour*. The immense alleviation given to the study of a language by such a grammar must be self-evident to everyone.

(2). I established rules for the formation of new words, and at the same time reduced to a very small compass the list of words absolutely necessary to be learned, without, however, depriving the language of the means of becoming a rich one. On the contrary, thanks to the possibility of forming from one root·

word any number of compounds, expressive of every conceivable shade of id. a, I made it the richest of the rich amongst modern tongues. This I accomplished by the introduction of numerous prefixes and suffixes, by whose aid the student is enabled to create new words for himself, without the necessity of having previously to learn them. For example :—

(1). The prefix *mal* denotes the direct opposite of any idea. If, for instance, we know the word for " good," *bon'a*, we can immediately form that for " bad," *mal'bon'a*, and hence the necessity of a special word for " bad " is obviated. In like manner, *alt'a*, " high," " tall," *mal'al'ta*, " low," " short " ; *estim'i*, " to respect," *mal'estim'i*, " to despise," etc. Consequently, if one has learned this single word *mal* he is relieved of learning a long string of words such as " hard," (premising that he knows " soft,") " cold," " old," " dirty," " distant," " darkness," " shame," " to hate," etc., etc.

(2). The suffix *in* marks the feminine gender, and thus if we know the word " brother," *frat'o*, we can form " sister," *frat'in'o* ; so also, " father," *patr'o* ; " mother," *patr'in'o*. By this device words like " grandmother," " bride," " girl," " hen," " cow," etc., are done away with.

(3). The suffix *il* indicates an instrument for a given purpose, *e.g.*, *tranĉ'i*, " to cut," *tranĉ'il'o*, " a knife " ; so words like " comb," " axe," " bell," etc., are rendered unnecessary.

In the same manner are employed many other affixes—some fifty in all—which the reader will find in the vocabulary. Moreover, as I have laid it down as a general rule that every word already regarded as international—the so-called " foreign " words, for example—undergoes no change in my language, except such as may be necessary to bring it into conformity with the international orthography, innumerable words become superfluous, *e.g.*, "locomotive," "telegraph." "nerve," "temperature," "centre," "form," "public,." "platinum," "figure," "waggon," "comedy," and hundreds more.

By the help of these rules, and others, which will be found in the grammar, the language is rendered so exceedingly simple that the whole labour in learning consists in committing to memory some 3,000 words—which number includes all the grammatical inflexions, prefixes, etc. With the assistance of the rules given in the grammar, anyone of ordinary intellectual capacity may form for himself all the words, expressions, and idioms in ordinary use. Even these 3,000 words, as will be shown directly, are so chosen that the learning them offers no difficulty to a well-educated person.

Thus the acquirement of this rich, mellifluous, universally-comprehensible language is not a matter of years of a laborious study, but the mere light amusement of a few days.

Problem No. 2.

The solution of the second problem was effected thus :—

(1). I introduced a complete dismemberment of ideas into independent words, so that the whole language consists, not of words in different states of grammatical inflexion, but of unchangeable words. If the reader will turn to one of the pages of this book written in my language, he will perceive that each word always retains its original unalterable form—namely, that under which it appears in the vocabulary. The various grammatical inflexions, the reciprocal relations of the members of a sentence, arc expressed by the junction of immutable syllables.

But the structure of such a synthetic language being altogether strange to the chief European nations, and consequently difficult for them to become accustomed to, I have adapted this principle of dismemberment to the spirit of the European languages, in such a manner that anyone learning my tongue from grammar alone, without having previously read this introduction—which is quite unnecessary for the learner—will never perceive that the structure of the language differs in any respect from that of his mother-tongue. So, for example, the derivation of *frat'in'o*, which is in reality a compound of *frat* "child of the same parents as one's self," *in* "female," *o* "an entity," "that which exists," *i.e.*, "that which exists as a female child of the same parents as one's self " = " a sister,"—is explained by the grammar thus : the root for " brother " is *frat*, the termination of substantives in the nominative case is *o*, hence *frat'o* is the equivalent of "brother"; the feminine gender is formed by the suffix *in*, hence *frat'in'o* = "sister." (The little strokes between certain letters are added in accordance with a rule of the grammar, which requires their insertion between each component part of every complete word). Thus the learner experiences no difficulty, and never even imagines that what he calls terminations, suffixes, etc., are complete and independent words, which always keep their own proper significations, whether placed at the beginning or end of a word, in the middle, or alone. The result of this construction of the language is that everything written in it can be immediately and perfectly understood by the help of the vocabulary—or even almost without it—by anyone who has not only not learnt the language before, but even has never heard of its very existence.

Let me illustrate this by an example :—I am amongst Englishmen, and have not the slightest knowledge of the English language ; I am absolutely in need of making myself understood, and write in the international tongue, maybe, as follows :—

Mi ne sci'as kie mi las'is la baston'o'n ; ĉu vi ĝin ne vid'is ?

I hold out to one of the strangers an International English vocabulary, and point to the title, where the following sentence appears in large letters :—" Everything written in the international language can be translated by the help of this vocabulary. If several words together express but a single idea, they are written as one word, but separated by commas ; *e.g.*, *frat'in'o*, though a single idea, is yet composed of three words, which must be looked for separately in the vocabulary." If my companion has never heard of the international language he will probably favour me at first with a vacant stare, will then take the paper offered to him, and, searching for the words in the vocabulary, as directed, will make out something of this kind :—

Mi	*mi*	= I	I
ne	*ne*	= not	not
sci'as	*sci*	= know	do know
	as	= sign of the present tense	
kie	*kie*	= where	where
mi	*mi*	= I	I
lasis	*las*	= leave	have left
	is	= sign of the past tense	
la	*la*	= the	the
baston'o'n ;	*baston*	= stick	stick ;
	o	= sign of a substantive	
	n	= sign of the objective case	

ĉu	*ĉu*	= whether, if, employed in questions	}	whether
vi	*vi*	= you, thou	}	you
ĝin	*ĝi*	= it, this	}	it
	n	= sign of the objective case		
ne	*ne*	= not	}	not
vid'is ?	*vid*	= see	}	have seen ?
	is	— sign of the past tense		

And thus the Englishman will easily understand what it is I desire. If he wishes to reply, I show him an English-International vocabulary, on which are printed these words:—" To express anything by means of this vocabulary, in the international language, look for the words required in the vocabulary itself; and for the terminations necessary to distinguish the grammatical forms look in the grammatical appendix, under the respective headings of the parts of speech which you desire to express." Since the explanation of the whole grammatical structure of the language is comprised in a few lines—as a glance at the grammar will show—the finding of the required terminations occupies no longer time than the turning up a word in the dictionary.

I would now direct the attention of my readers to another matter, at first sight a trifling one. but, in truth, of immense importance. Everyone knows the impossibility of communicating intelligibly with a foreigner by the aid of even the best of dictionaries, if one have no previous acquaintance with the language. In order to find any given word in a dictionary, we must know its derivation, for when words are arranged in sentences, nearly every one of them undergoes some grammatical change. After this alteration, a word often bears not the least resemblance to its primary form, so that without knowing something of the language beforehand, we are able to find hardly any of the words occurring in a given phrase, and even those we do find will give no connected sense. Suppose, for example, I had written the simple sentence adduced above in German : "Ich weiss nicht wo ich den Stock gelassen habe ; haben Sie ihn nicht gesehen ?" Anyone who did not speak or understand German, after searching for each word separately in a dictionary, would produce the following farrago of nonsense : "I ; white ; not ; where ; I ;— ; stick ; dispassionate ; property ; to have ; she, they, you ;— ; not ;— ?" I need scarcely point out that a lexicon of a modern language is usually a volume of a certain bulk, and the search for any number of words one by one is in itself a most laborious undertaking, not to speak of the different significations attaching to the same word, amongst which there is but a bare possibility of the student selecting the right one. The international vocabulary, owing to the highly synthetic structure of the language, is a mere leaflet, which one might carry in one's note book, or the waistcoat-pocket.

Granted that we *had* a language with a grammar simplified to the utmost, and whose every word had a definite fixed meaning, the person addressed would require not only to have beforehand some knowledge of the grammar, to be able, even with the vocabulary at hand, to understand anything addressed to him, but would also need some previous acquaintance with the vocabulary itself, in order to be able to distinguish between the primitive word and its grammatically-altered derivatives. The utility, again, of such a language would wholly depend upon the number of its adepts, for when sitting, for instance, in a railway-carriage, and wishing to ask a fellow-traveller "How long do we stop at — ?" it is scarcely to be expected that he will undertake to learn the grammar of the language before replying! By using, on the other hand, the international language, we are set in possibility of communicating directly with a person of any nationality, even though he may never have heard of the existence of the language before.

Anything whatever, written in the international tongue, can be translated, without difficulty, by means of the vocabulary alone, no previous study being requisite. The reader may easily convince himself of the truth of this assertion by experimenting for himself with the specimens of the language appended to this pamphlet. A person of good education will seldom need to refer to the vocabulary, a linguist scarcely at all.

Let us suppose that you have to write to a Spaniard, who neither knows your language nor you his. You think that probably he has never heard of the international tongue. No matter, write boldly to him in that language, and be sure he will understand you perfectly. The complete vocabulary required for everyday use, being but a single sheet of paper, can be bought for a few pence, in any language you please, easily enclosed in the smallest envelope, and forwarded with your letter. The person to whom it is addressed will without doubt understand what you have written, the vocabulary being not only a clue to, but a complete explanation of your letter. The wonderful power of combination possessed by the words of the international language renders this lilliputian lexicon amply sufficient for the expression of every want of daily life; but words seldom met with, technical terms, and foreign words familiar to all nations, as "tobacco," "theatre," "fabric," etc., are not included in it. If such words, therefore, are needed, and it is impossible to express them by some equiva lent terms, the larger vocabulary must be consulted

(2). It has now been shown how, by means of the peculiar structure of the international tongue, anyone may enter into an intelligible correspondence with another person of a different nationality. The sole drawback, until the language becomes more widely known, is the necessity under which the writer is placed of waiting until the person addressed shall have analysed his thoughts. In order to remove this obstacle as far as practicable, at least for persons of education, recourse was had to the following expedient. Such words as are common to the languages of all civilised peoples, together with the so-called "foreign" words and technical terms, were left unaltered. If a word has a different sound in different languages, that sound has been chosen which is common to at least two or three of the most important European tongues, or which, if found in one language only, has become familiar to other nations. When the required word has a different sound in every language, some word was sought for, having only a relative likeness in meaning to the other, or one which, though seldom used, is yet well known to the leading nations, e.g., the word for "near" is different in every European language, but if one consider for a moment the word "proximus" (nearest), it will be noticed that some modified form of the word is in use in all important tongues. If, then, I call "near" *proksim*, the meaning will be apparent to every educated man. In other emergencies words were drawn from the Latin, as being a quasi-international language. Deviations from these rules were only made in exceptional cases, as for the avoidance of homonyms, simplicity of orthography, etc. In this manner, being in communication with a European of fair education, who has never learnt the international tongue, one may make sure of being immediately understood, without the person addressed having to refer continually to the vocabulary.

In order that the reader may prove for himself the truth of all that has been set forth above, two specimens of the international language are subjoined.*

PATR′O NI′A.

Patr′o ni′a, kiu est′as en la ĉiel′o, sankt′a est′u Vi′a nom′o, ven′u reĝ′ec′o Vi′a, est′u vol′o Vi′a, kiel en la ĉiel′o, tiel ankaŭ sur la ter′o. Pan′o′n ni′a′n ĉiu′tag′a′n don′u al ni hodiaŭ, kaj pardon′u al ni ŝuld′o′j′n ni′aj′n, kiel ni ankaŭ pardon′as al ni′a′j ŝuld′ant′o′j ; ne konduku ni′n en tent′o′n ; sed liber′ig′u ni′n de la mal′vera, ĉar Vi′a est′as la regad′o, la fort′o, kaj la gloro eterne. Amen !

EL LA BIBLI′O.

Je la komenc′o Di′o kre′is la ter′o′n kaj la ĉiel′o′n. Kaj la ter′o est′is sen′form′a kaj dezert′a, kaj mal′lum′o est′is super la profund′a′ĵo, kaj la anim′o de Di′o si′n port′is super la akv′o. Kaj Di′o dir′is : est′u lum′o ; kaj far′iĝ′is lum′o. Kaj Di′o vid′is la lum′o′n ke ĝi est′as bon′a, kaj nom′is Di′o la lum′o′n tag′o, kaj la mal′lum′o′n Li nom′is nokt′o. Kaj est′is vesper′o, kaj est′is maten′o—unu tag′o. Kaj Di′o dir′is : est′u firm′aĵ′o inter la akv′o, kaj ĝi apart′ig′u akv′on de akv′o. Kaj Di′o kre′is la firm′aĵ′o′n kaj apart′ig′is la akv′o′n kiu est′as sub la firm′aĵ′o, de la akv′o kiu est′as super la firm′aĵ′o ; kaj far′iĝ′is tiel. Kaj Di′o nom′is la firm′-aĵ′o′n ĉiel′o. Kaj est′is vesper′o, kaj est′is maten′o— la du′a tag′o. Kaj Di′o dir′is : kolekt′u sin la akv′o de sub la ĉiel′o unu lok′o′n, kaj montr′u si′r sek′aĵ′o ; kaj far′iĝ′is tiel. Kaj Di′o nom′is la sek′aĵ′o′n ter′o, kaj la kolekt′o′j′n de la akv′o Li nom′is mar′o′j.

* In correspondence with persons who have learnt the language, as well as in works written for them exclusively, the commas, separating parts of words, are omitted.

ADVICE TO THE STUDENT.

1. The lessons, etc., in this text-book are arranged to meet what must be the great aims of an International language, viz. :

(1). To read it with facility.
(2). To speak it with facility.
(3). To write it with facility.

2. And, in order to fulfil these ends, the Lessons have been divided into three sections, namely :— Exercises, Conversations, and Specimens of Correspondence. All these can be taken in their order, but there is nothing to prevent a student from working at the Conversations before the Exercises (Section I.) have been finished. The Correspondence (Section III.), however, should not be attempted until the Exercises and Conversations are thoroughly mastered.

3. In order to facilitate the study of the language, I would advise the student to give his careful attention to the following suggestions :—

4. Do not begin the Exercises until the sound value of every letter in the Alphabet is thoroughly mastered.

5. Even when this point is attained, let no day pass without reading *aloud* the words of, at least, one Exercise; this for three reasons—firstly, as an exercise in pronunciation; secondly, to accustom the ear to the sound of the words; thirdly, for a better remembering of the words, one sense here materially helping the other.

6. Keep well before the mind, for this end, the fact that the language is phonetic, one letter having always and everywhere one sound, and, finally, remember there are no silent letters.

7. In mentioning the letters it is well to give them the names by which they are universally known; this is done by adding an *O* to each consonant. Thus the

name of B is bo, D is do, M is mo, R is ro, $\hat{S}$ is ŝho, Z is zo, etc., etc. This gives the Alphabet its own proper characteristic, which is totally distinct from the alphabets of all other languages.

8. Learn the Grammatical Terminations which precede the Grammar proper. "Hasten slowly," do not be in too great a hurry, proceed step by step. Too great haste only retards progress.

9. Recapitulate occasionally. When you finish the first 10 Lessons repeat them ; do the same when you finish Lesson 20, and finally have a repetition of the whole When you do this thoroughly you have a "working capital" of close on 700 or 800 words.

10. Moreover, if you act in this way, the remaining Sections (II. and III.) will present no difficulty.

11. Having finished the Exercises, I would suggest that the student subscribe to one of the journals (of which there are now at least ten published) printed for the propagation of the language. Some of these are printed entirely in Esperanto, others in French and Esperanto. An English Esperanto monthly is in preparation.

12. If you wish to correspond in the language, you should obtain the Annual Universal address book issued by Dr. Zamenhof, an application form for which can be had by applying to the Esperanto Club. By giving one hour each day to the language, at the end of a few weeks you will find no difficulty in this. And remember, by means of "Esperanto," your correspondence need not be limited to one or two countries. Practically, by the means of this language, your field is boundless for this purpose.

13. Every Esperantist should obtain and carefully study Dr. Zamenhof's "*Fundamenta Krestomatio,*" which is the guide to style, and contains the larger part of Dr. Zamenhof's own writings.

SYNOPSIS OF THE GRAMMAR OF ESPERANTO.

GRAMMATICAL TERMINATIONS.

I final denotes always the infinitive. *Ami*, to love.

AS	,,	,,	,,	,, present tense. *Mi amas*, love.
IS	,,	,,	,,	,, past tense. *Vi amis*, you loved.
OS	,,	,,	,,	,, future tense *Ili amos*, they will love.
US	,,	,,	,,	,, conditional. *Li amus*, he should or would love.
U	,,	,,	,,	,, imperative. *Amu*, love ; *li amu*, let him love
ANTA*	,,	,,	,,	,, present participle (active) *Amanta*, loving.
INTA	,,	,,	,,	,, past participle (active). *Aminta*, having loved.
ONTA	,,	,,	,,	,, future participle (active). *Amonta*, about to love.
ATA	,,	,,	,,	,, present participle (passive). *Amata*, being loved.
ITA	,,	,,	,,	,, past participle (passive). *Amita*, having been loved.
OTA	,,	,,	,,	,, future participle (passive). *Amota*, about to be loved.
O	,,	,,	,,	,, noun. *Patro*, father.
A	,,	,,	,,	,, adjective. *Patra*, paternal.
E	,,	,,	,,	,, adverb. *Patrè*, paternally.
J	,,	,,	,,	,, plur. *Bonaj patroj*, good fathers.
N			,,	,, objective (accusative) case. and the direction towards which one goes *Mi trovis la libron*, I found the book. *Ŝi iras Londonon*, she goes to London.

---

* The final " A " of participles is changed to " E " when used adverbially, as *amante*, by (or in) loving.

PART I.—THE ESPERANTO GRAMMAR.

The Alphabet.

1. There are twenty-eight letters in the alphabet, viz. :—

Aa,	Dd,	Ĝĝ,	Jj,	Mm,	Rr,	Uu,
Bb,	Ee,	Hh,	Ĵĵ,	Nn,	Ss,	Ŭŭ,
Cc,	Ff,	Ĥĥ,	Kk,	Oo,	Ŝŝ,	Vv,
Ĉĉ,	Gg,	Ii,	Ll,	Pp,	Tt,	Zz.

2. With the exception of the following, these letters are pronounced exactly as in English :—

A   is always pronounced as " a " in father.
E   "   "   "   " " e " in they.
I   "   "   " " ee " in seen.
O   "   "   "   " " o " in so.
U   "   "   "   " " u " in rule.
C   "   "   " " ts " in bits.
Ĉ   "   "   " " ch " in church.
G   "   "   " " g " in good.
Ĝ   "   "   " " g " in gem.
Ĥ   "   "   " " ch " in loch.
J   "   "   " " y " in yes.
Ĵ   "   "   " " s " in vision.
S   "   "   " " s " in basin, never like " s " in rose.
Ŝ   "   "   " " sh " in she.
Aŭ   "   "   " " ow " in how.
Aj   "   "   " " i " in nigh.
Oj   "   "   " " oy " in boy.
Eŭ   "   "   " " eh-oo " as in the words " they who."
Ej   "   "   " " ayi " in saying.
Uj   "   "   "   " " ui " in ruin.

NOTE.—Dr. Zamenhof permits the substitution of the letter " h " for the accent, in all cases of ch, gh, hh, jh, and sh.

3. The sound of the letters is always the same, whether initial, medial or final. " One letter one sound."

4. There are no silent letters in Esperanto ; every letter must be sounded separately, even in the case of the double letters, *Aj*, *Aŭ* and *Oj*, the pronunciation of which is given. " H " is never silent.

5. Esperanto being a phonetic language, every word is read exactly as it is written, and written as read.

Dume = " doo-may," not " doom." *Iel* = " ee-ale," not " eel."

Traire = " trah-ee-ray," not " tra-ire." *Fingringo* = feen-green-go, not fing-gring-o (treat " ing " always after this model).

The Accent.

1. Every word in Esperanto is accented on the penultimate (the last syllable but one). Hence this syllable must be well marked, raising the voice on it, and not on the final syllable. Even in words of two syllables the accent must be strong, distinct and clear upon the first. This is called the " tonic " accent.

2. This, however, does not mean that the other syllables should be slurred or pronounced carelessly. Every syllable must get its full sound-value, but the neglect of the tonic accent would tend, in a great measure, to rob the language of an essential part of its beauty and euphony

Compound Words.

These are formed by the junction of words, much the same as in English. In Esperanto the principal word is always placed last, this word taking the termination determining which part of speech it is.

Antaŭ, before, *Vid'*, see.   *Antaŭvidi*, to foresee (verb).
Griz, grey, *Har'*, hair.   *Grizhara*, greyhaired (adj).
Vapor, steam, *Ŝip'*, ship.   *Vaporŝipo*, steamship (noun`.

The grammatical terminations " i," " a," " o," are regarded as independent words in such cases. In elementary work, or in corresponding with learners, the different parts of compound words are divided by perpendicular or sloping bars ', as *Vapor'ŝip'o, Griz'har'a, Antaŭ'vid'i.*

Foreign Words.

1. By " foreign words " we understand a large class of words which most languages receive from a common source.

2. In Esperanto these words retain their original form, undergoing no change except only so far as they are subject to its orthographical system and rules.

Mikrofono, Microphone.	*Teatro*, Theatre.
Mikrofona, Microphonic.	*Teatra*, Theatrical.
Mikrofone, Microphonically.	*Teatre*, Theatrically.

3. As will be seen from these examples, the derived words—*Mikrofona, mikrofone, teatra, teatre,* always originate or spring from the root of the primary word, *mikrofon', teatr'.*

Elision.

1. Elision is not common in Esperanto; its use is rather to be avoided than followed.

2. The only letters that may be elided are the " a " of the article and the " o " of nouns (in the singular). When elision does take place, an apostrophe is used to denote the dropped letter. *La domo de l'mastro,* the house of the master; or, the master's house. *Ŝiller' estis glora poeto;* Schiller was a glorious poet.

3. In no case is elision obligatory.

Interrogation.

Ĉu denotes an interrogation, as *Ĉu li legas?* Does he read? It is also used in indirect questions, when it means "whether."

Negation.

As in English, double negatives must not be used.

Mi nenion trovis, I found nothing.

Ŝi neniun vidis en la palaco, she saw no one in the palace.

Direction.

In answers to questions beginning with "*Kien,*" "where" (meaning direction), the word or words must have the termination of the objective. As, *Kien li iras?* Where does he go? (Where is he going?) *Li iras ĝardenon—Londonon.* He goes (or is going) to a garden—to London.

PARTS OF SPEECH.

The Article.

1. There is no indefinite article in Esperanto.
It is contained in the Noun (as in Latin) according as the sense does or does not require it, as:

Rozo estas floro, a rose is a flower.
Patro kaj frato, father and brother.

2. The definite article is *La,* the. (It is invariable).

La patro, the father. *La patrino,* the mother.
La tablo, the table. *La patroj,* the fathers.
La birdoj estas sur la arbo, the birds are on the tree.

3. The definite article is never used in Esperanto before proper names, as :

Unuigitaj Ŝtatoj Amerikaj. The United States of America.

Francujo estas pli varma ol Anglujo.* France is warmer than England.

4. The definite article is used in Esperanto before nouns denoting the totality of persons or things represented, as

La homo estas mortema, man is mortal.

The Noun.

1. The noun, in Esperanto, invariably ends in " o," as :

Patro, father. *Patrino,* mother. *Arbo,* tree.

2. The plural is formed by adding "j" (pron. "y") to the singular, as :

Patroj, fathers. *Patrinoj,* mothers. *Arboj,* trees.

3. The objective case (sometimes named the Accusative) is formed by adding "n" to the singular or plural, as :

Mi havas floron, birdon kaj libron.
I have a flower, a bird and a book.
Mi havas florojn birdojn kaj librojn.
I have flowers, birds and books.

This form of the objective is not used in English, but as Esperanto is a language to be used by all nations, and having to unite clearness with simplicity, it had to be so formed that however the words in a sentence may be arranged, the subject and object cannot be read one for another.†

---

* Alternative forms are *Franclando, Anglolando.*
† For a special Note on the use of the Accusative see p. 166.

4. Possession is denoted as follows :—

La domo de la patro, the father's house.
La libro de la patrino, the mother's book.
La ĉapelo de Johano, John's hat.

5. The direction, or place towards which one goes, also takes the sign of the objective case, " n," as ·

Mi iras Romon, I go to Rome. *La hundo saltis sur la liton,* the dog jumped on (to) the bed. (He was not on the bed when he jumped, he was on the floor or elsewhere, and from there he jumped on to the bed).

But, *La hundo saltis sur la lito* means he was on the bed, and then jumped about on it.

6. The feminine is formed by inserting—*in*—before the termination *o* or *oj,* as : *patro, patr-in-o,* father, mother.

Edzo, edz-in-o, husband, wife. *Koko, kok-in-o,* cock, hen.

Mi vidis la edzon kaj la edzinon, I saw the husband and the wife.

7. " N " is also used in words signifying date. *Li venis lundon,* he came (on) Monday.

8. In words expressing weight, measure, price and duration " N " is likewise added, as *Ŝi kantis du horojn,* she sang (for) 2 hours.

The Adjective.

1. All adjectives, and participles when used as adjectives, end in " a," as :

Forta, strong. *Riĉa,* rich. *Brava,* brave.
La bona patro, la bela patrino kaj la juna filo (sing).

The good father, the beautiful mother and the young son.

La bonaj patroj, la belaj patrinoj kaj la junaj filoj (plur.).

The good fathers, the beautiful mothers and the young sons.

2. If an adjective qualifies or refers to a noun in the objective case such adjective must also take the sign of that case, " n," as :

Mi trovis junan birdon en la ĝardeno.
I found a young bird in the garden.
Mi aĉetis du ĉarmajn librojn.
I bought two charming books.

3. The adjective may precede or follow the noun it qualifies, as :

Mi havas novan ĉapelon, or *mi havas ĉapelon novan,* I have a new hat.

4. As already stated, participial adjectives, that is participles used as adjectives, follow the above rules.

Amanta amiko, a loving friend. *Amantaj amikoj,* loving friends.

Adjectives must never be used as adverbs, nor adverbs as adjectives.

Comparison of Adjectives.

1. Adjectives are compared as follows :—

The comparative of equality is, *tiel—kiel,* as— as. (1).

The comparative of superiority is, *pli—ol,* more— than. (2).

The comparative of inferiority is, *malpli—ol,* less— than. (3).

Vi estas tiel forta kiel li. You are as strong as he. (1).

Vi estas pli forta ol li. You are stronger than he (2).

Vi estas malpli forta ol li   You are less stron··
(weaker) than he.   (3).

2. The superlative of superiority is *la plej* (—*el*) the
most (—of, in, amongst).   (4).

The superlative of inferiority is *la malplej* (—*el*) the
least (—of, in, amongst).   (5).

Li estas la plej kuraĝa homo en la mondo (el ni ĉiuj). (4).
He is the most courageous man in the world
(amongst us all).

Mi estas la piej riĉa el ĉiuj.   (4).
I am the richest of all.

Mi estas la malplej forta el ni.   (5).
I am the least strong (weakest) amongst us.

3. The superlative absolute is indicated by " *tre*,"
" very."

Mia patro estas tre riĉa kaj tre feliĉa.
My father is very rich and very happy.

Numerals.

1. The cardinal numbers are : *Unu* (1), *du* (2), *tri*
(3), *kvar* (4), *kvin* (5), *ses* (6), *sep* (7), *ok* (8), *naŭ* (9),
dek (10), *cent* (100), *mil* (1000).

2. The tens and hundreds are formed by the aid
of the numbers preceding : *Dek* (10) or *cent* (100), as
dudek (20), *tridek* (30), *sesdek* (60), *naŭdek* (90),
kvarcent (400), *kvincent* (500), *naŭcent* (900).

3. The intermediate numbers between 10 and 100
are formed as follows : *Dek-du* (12), *dek-sep* (17),
dek-naŭ (19), *tridek-sep* (37), *sepdek-kvin* (75), *naŭcent*
tridek-du (932), *sepcent okdek-unu* (781), *mil naŭcent tri*
(1903).

The use of the hyphen is not obligatory.

4. Ordinals are formed from the corresponding
cardinals by adding the termination "a" of adjectives.

Unua (first), *kvara* (fourth), *dek-unua* (eleventh),
kvindek-tria (fifty-third), *ducent-dudek-tria* (two hundred
and twenty-third), *mil naŭcent-tria* (1903 A.D.).

5. If the cardinal number is composed of different numbers, "a" is added to the last only.

6. Ordinals being in reality adjectives, they follow the rules of adjectives as to case and number, as :

Donu al li la unuan, kaj prenu la kvaran.

Give him the first and take the fourth.

7. Cardinals undergo no change.

8. Fractional numbers are formed by adding "on" to the cardinals, and then adding "o" or "a" according as they are nouns or adjectives. *La centona parto de la mono,* the hundredth part of the money. *Kvar estas la duono de ok,* four is the half of eight. *Tri okonoj,* three eighths ($\frac{3}{8}$). *Kvin seponoj,* five-sevenths ($\frac{5}{7}$).

9. Multiples are formed by adding "obl" to the cardinals, and then adding "o" or "a" as in fractionals, to mark the noun or adjective. *Duobla,* double. *Triobla,* triple. *Sepobla,* sevenfold.

10. Collectives are formed by adding "op" to the cardinals, and then adding "a" or "e" according as they are adjectives or adverbs. *Duope,* by twos, *Dekope,* by tens.

11. Once, twice, thrice, etc., are formed by adding the word "foje" to the cardinals, as *Unufoje,* once. *Dufoje,* twice. *Trifoje,* thrice, etc.

Personal Pronouns.

1. The personal pronouns are : *Mi,* I. *Vi,* thou,* you. *Li,* he. *Ŝi,* she. *Ĝi,* it. *Ni,* we. *Ili,* they.

Oni, they, we, people, it. This is the French "on."

Si, self, reflexive pronoun, of all genders and numbers. This pronoun is naturally of the third person.

2. They form the objective case in the same way as nouns : *Min,* me. *Vin,* you. *Lin,* him. *Ŝin,* her. *Ĝin,* it. *Nin,* us. *Ilin,* them.

---

* "Thou" in familiar address is represented by " *Ci,*" but this is rarely used in Esperanto.

Mi trovis lin en la ĝardeno kun mia patro.
I found him in the garden with my father.
Ŝi vidis nin en la dormoĉambro.
She saw us in the bedroom.
Oni diras, "per mono oni povas aĉeti ĉion."
They say (it is said) · "By means of money one can buy everything."

3. *Ĝi* (it) is used, as in English, to represent things, and also persons and animals, the name of which does not reveal the sex.

La infano ploras, ĉar ĝi estas malsata.
The infant cries, because it is hungry.

4. Before impersonal (sometimes named unipersonal) verbs *Ĝi* is understood. *Neĝas*, it snows. *Pluvis*, it rained. *Tondros*, it will thunder. *Estas necese manĝi*, it is necessary to eat.

Possessive Pronouns.

1. The possessive pronouns (which are essentially adjectives) are formed from the corresponding personal pronouns by adding "a" to them, as: *Mia*, my, mine. *Via*, your, yours. *Lia*, his. *Ŝia*, her, hers. *Ĝia*, its. *Nia*, our, ours. *Ilia*, their, theirs.

Mia patro kaj via frato estis en la domo.
My father and your brother were in the house.

2. In sentences like the following these possessives may, or may not, be preceded by the definite article "la," as:

Mia fratino estas pli bela ol (la) via.
My sister is more beautiful than yours.

3. They form the objective case in the same way as nouns and adjectives, that is, by the addition of "n."

Ili vidis vian fraton kaj mian fratinon.
They saw your brother and my sister.

4. Also, like nouns and adjectives, they form their plurals by adding "ꭹ" to the singular.

Mi trovis miajn librojn en la skatolo.

I found my books in the box.

Sia, Lia, etc.

1. The correct use of these possessives demands attention. They must not be used indiscriminately; each has its distinct and separate *rôle*. In such (English) sentences as: "John saw my father and his friend," there is a doubt whose "friend" is meant. Is it "John's" friend or the "father's" that is meant?

2. In Esperanto there can be no such ambiguity. (*a*). *Johano vidis mian patron kaj* lian *amikon*. (*b*). *Johano vidis mian patron kaj sian amikon*. Now, the rule is *Sia* can only refer to the *subject* of the sentence or proposition in which it occurs. Therefore in (*a*), *Johano* being the subject, *lian* cannot refer to him, but to the father, "John saw my father and his (the father's) friend." In (*b*), again taking the rule, *Sian* does refer to Johano; consequently it means "John saw my father and his (John's) friend." *Petro skribis al Johano, ke li alkonduku al li* $\left\{ \begin{array}{l} lian \\ sian \end{array} \right\}$ *ĉevalon*. In this example *lian* refers to Peter's horse, because Peter is *not* the subject of proposition. *Sian*, on the contrary, *does* refer to the subject (li) of the proposition, therefore it is John's horse is meant. By the correct use of these pronouns all ambiguity is avoided.

The Verb (ACTIVE VOICE).

1. There is no such thing as an irregular verb in Esperanto. Therefore when the pupil has learned the conjugation of one verb, he knows the conjugation of every verb in the language.

2. *I*, final, denotes the infinitive mood, as:

Ami, to love. *Doni*, to give. *Havi*,* to have.
As, final, denotes the present tense of verbs.
Mi amas, I love. *Li amas*, he loves, etc.
Is, final, denotes the past tense of verbs.
Vi amis, you loved. *Ili amis*, they loved, etc.
Os, final, denotes the future tense of verbs.
Ŝi amos, she will love. *Ĝi amos*, it will love, etc.
Us, final, denotes the conditional mood of verbs.
Mi amus, I should or would love, etc.
U, final, denotes the imperative mood of verbs.
Amu, love. *Li, ŝi, ĝi, finu*, let him, her, it finish.
Ni, ili finu, let us, let them finish.

3. This form in *U* is also used for the subjunctive mood, as *ke mi amu*, that I may love, etc.

4. The personal pronouns must always be expressed before the verb, except in the case of impersonal verbs.

Participles.

1. The active voice has three participles which help to form the perfect tenses of verbs.

2. *Anta* final, denotes the present participle (active) It is the same as the English participle in—ing.

Amanta, loving. *Leganta*, reading.

Inta, final, denotes the past participle (active).

It is the same as the English participle, in—ed, en, etc.

Aminta, having loved, *Skribinta*, having written.

---

* Note that in Esperanto "have" is not an auxiliary, but always a principal, active verb, denoting possession and therefore governs the objective case.

Onta, final, denotes the future participle.

This has no participial equivalent in English.

Mi estas amonta, I am about to love.

3. These participles can be used as nouns, adjectives, and adverbs, in which case they take the distinctive terminations of these parts of speech, and are subject to the same rules as to number and case.

Amanta amiko, a loving friend (participial adjective).

Legante ni lernas, by reading, we learn (participial adverb).

La legonto, the person (who is) about to read (participial noun).

4. When *Esti*, to be, is used to form the compound tenses, it is always translated as follows :—

*Mi est*AS *am*ANTA,	I am loving.
*Mi est*AS *am*INTA,	I have loved.
*Mi est*AS *am*ONTA,	I am about to love.
*Mi est*IS *am*ANTA,	I was loving.
*Mi est*IS *am*INTA,	I had loved.
*Mi est*IS *am*ONTA,	I was about to love.
*Mi est*OS *am*ANTA,	I shall be loving.
*Mi est*OS *am*INTA,	I shall have loved.
*Mi est*OS *am*ONTA,	I shall be about to love.

5. As will be seen from the above examples the present participle of the active verb, preceded by the different parts of *Esti*, is used to form the "progressive" tenses, as :

Mi estas amanta, I am loving.

Mi estis amanta, I was loving.

Mi estos skribanta, I shall be writing. But these forms are avoided as far as possible in Esperanto, the simpler forms being used—*Mi amas, mi amis, mi amos*.

The Passive Voice.

1. In addition to the three participles of the active verb, there are also three participles for the passive form of the verb.

2. *Ata,* final, denotes the present participle (passive).
Amata, loved (now). *Skribata,* written (now).
Ita, final, denotes the past participle (passive).
Amita, been loved. *Skribita,* been written.
Ota, final, denotes the future participle (passive).
Amota, about to be loved.
Skribota, about to be written.

3. In the same way as participles of the active verb, these participles may be used as nouns, adjectives, and adverbs, and are subject to the same rules.

4. The passive voice is formed by the different part of Esti joined to one of the passive participles.

5. The following examples illustrate this :

*Mi est*AS *am*ATA,	I am loved.
*Mi est*AS *am*ITA,	I have been loved.
*Mi est*AS *am*OTA,	I am about to be loved.
*Mi est*IS *am*ATA,	I was loved.
*Mi est*IS *am*ITA,	I had been loved.
*Mi est*IS *am*OTA,	I was about to be loved.
*Mi est*OS *am*ATA,	I shall be loved.
*Mi est*OS *am*ITA,	I shall have been loved.
*Mi est*OS *am*OTA,	I shall be about to be loved.

6. The preposition "by" which precedes the complement of the passive voice is translated by "de."
Li estas amata de ĉiuj.
He is (being) loved by all.

Ŝi estis amata de sia patrino.
She was loved by her mother.

7. These participles are sometimes used as adverbs in the same way as the active participles. The "a" final is then changed to "e," but they do not take the termination "j" of the plural.

Batate de la patro, la infano ekploris.
Being beaten by the father, the child began to weep.

Prepositions.

1, Prepositions in Esperanto govern the nominative case, and not the objective case, as in English.

Li kuris al ni, he ran to us.

La hundo estas en la ĉambro, the dog is in the room.

2. Every preposition has a fixed and definite meaning. Hence the pupil must guard against translating the English preposition by its *apparent* corresponding one in Esperanto. To do so would be the source of very grave errors.

3. Let the pupil, then, be careful to take always that preposition, the sense of which in Esperanto expresses clearly the idea he wishes to express.

4. If a preposition is to be employed in a sentence where the choice is not definite from the sense of the phrase, then in such case use the preposition "Je," the only one in the language whose signification is not defined. In addition to this, an alternative course is open, namely, omit the preposition and use the objective case, when no ambiguity or confusion is likely to arise from doing so.

Li ĝojas je tio, or *Li ĝojas tion,* he rejoices at (over) that. *Mi ploras je via naiveco,* or *Mi ploras vian naivecon,* I weep at your simplicity.

5. The correct use of prepositions can best be learnt by reading works in Esperanto

6. List of the most common prepositions :

Apud,	near, at the side of.	*Per,*	by means of.
Dum,	during.	*Po,*	by (with numbers) at the rate of.
En,	in.		
Preter,	beside, beyond.	*Super,*	over, above.
Sen,	without.	*Sur,*	on, upon (resting on, touching).
Sub,	under, beneath.		
De,	of, from.	*Pro,*	for the sake of, on account of.
Kontraŭ,	against.		
Ĉe.	at.	*Al,*	to, towards (where one goes).
Inter,	between, among.	*Da,*	of (after words of number, weight, etc.)
Ĝis,	up to, until.		
Krom,	except, besides.		
Mulgraŭ,	in spite of.	*Ekster,*	outside, besides.
Post,	after, behind.	*Por,*	for, in favour of, in order to (before infinitives).
Laŭ,	according to.		
Anstalaŭ,	instead of.		
Antaŭ,	before, in front of.	*Tra,*	through.
Ĉirkaŭ,	about, around.	*Pri,*	{ about, concerning regarding, of.
Kun,	with, in company with.		
El,	from, out of.	*Trans,*	across.

Prepositions always precede their complement.

The Adverb.

1. There are two kinds of adverbs : (1), those which are derived from adjectives, nouns, etc. ; and (2) a class of simple words which are not derived, but which are, by nature, adverbs.

2. Derived adverbs always end in "e," as : *Bone,* well. *Ĉarme,* charmingly. *Rapide, malrapide,* quickly, slowly.

3. These are compared in the same way as adjectives. *Ŝi kuras tiel rapide kiel Johano.*

She runs as quickly as John.

Li kantas pli bone ol vi.
He sings better than you.
Vi kantas la plej ĉarme el ĉiuj.
You sing the most charmingly of all.

4. The other class of adverbs has no distinctive termination. Amongst the most important are the following :—

Almenaŭ,	at least.	*Iel,*	somehow, in some way, or manner.
Ambaŭ,	both.		
Ankaŭ,	also.		
Apenaŭ,	{ hardly. scarcely.	*Neniel,*	nohow, in no manner.
Aŭ,	or.	*Jam-ne,*	no —more.
Baldaŭ,	soon.	*Jen-Jen,*	sometimes— sometimes.
Ĉiam,	always,		
Ĉie,	everywhere.	*Ju pli ...* *des pli*	the more—the more.
Jam,	already.		
Kial,	why.	*Jus,*	just (now).
Kiam,	when.	*Ne,*	no, not.
Kie,	where.	*Tute ne,*	not at all.
Kiom,	{ how much. how many.	*Plu,*	more.
		Nek,	neither.
Nun,	now.	*Tuj,*	immediately.
Nur,	only.	*Tuj kiam,*	as soon as.
Preskaŭ,	nearly.	*Tiam,*	then.
Adiaŭ,	adieu.	*Tiam kiam,*	then when.
Kiel ujn,	however.	*For,*	forth, out.
Kie ajn,	wherever.	*Tiel,*	thus, so.
Kiam ajn,	whenever.	*Nenie,*	nowhere.
Troe,	excessively	*Ie,*	somewhere.
Treege,	exceedingly.	*Ĉiujare,*	yearly.
Ĉu-Ĉu,	whether— whether.	*Ĉiumonate,*	monthly.
		Ĉiutage,*	daily.
Eĉ,	even.		

* *Ĉiutage*, etc., are used in the adjectival form in such expressions as *Ĉiutaga gazeto*, a daily (everyday-ly) paper. Our common expression logically means a paper published during the hours of sunlight, not one published every day.

Adverbs, as a rule, immediately precede or follow the word to which they refer or qualify.

Ne and words used in the comparison of adverbs, such as *tre, pli, plej, malpli,* etc., always precede the word to which they relate or modify.

Conjunctions.

1. Conjunctions in Esperanto exercise no influence whatsoever over any words in a sentence. They are simply used to join words and sentences together.*

2. They always precede verbs, though not necessarily immediately preceding.

3. The following is a list of the chief conjunctions:

A lie,	otherwise.	*Sed,*	but.
Aŭ,	or.	*Tial,*	therefore.
Aŭ—aŭ,	either—or.	*Nek--nek,*	neither—nor.
Ĉar,	for, because.	*Do,*	then, indeed,
Dum,	while.		therefore.
Ĝis,	until, up to.	*Apenaŭ,*	scarcely.
Ja,	indeed, in fact.	*Se tamen,*	if however,
Ke,	that.		therefore.
Sekve,	consequently.	*Nome,*	that is to say,
Se,	if.		to wit, namely.
		Eĉ se,	even if.

K. t. p. or *k. c. = Kaj tiel plu, kaj cetera,* and so on, and so forth, etc.

T. e. = tio estas, that is, that is to say.

---

* "Antaŭ ol," " Anstataŭ " and " por " are generally followed by the infinitive mood.
" Por ke " is always followed by the imperative mood.

(PRONOUNS, ADJECTIVES, ADVERBS, AND CONJUNCTIVE ADVERBS).

Quality.	1. *ia* some kind of any kind of	10. *cia* each every every kind of	19. *kia* what a what kind of	28. *nenia* no (such) no kind of	37. *tia* such a such kind of
Motive.	2. *ial* for {some / any} {reason / cause}	11. *cial* or all reasons for every reason	20. *kial* why wherefore for what reason	29. *nenial* for no {reason / cause}	38. *tial* therefore
T me.	3. *iam* some / any} time ever	12. *ciam* always for all time	21. *kiam* when at what time	30. *neniam* never	39. *tiam* then at that time
P ace.	4. *ie* somewhere anywhere	13. *cie* everywhere	22. *kie* where in what place	31. *nenie* nowhere	40. *tie* there in that place
Manner.	5. *iel* somehow some way some manner anyhow	14. *ciel* every way all ways every manner	23. *kiel* how in hat manner	32. *neniel* no manner noho	41. *tiel* thus like (that) in that manner so

	6. ıes anyone's somebody's anybody's	15. ĉies each one's everyone's	24. kies whose	33. nenies nobody's no one's	42. ties such a one's that one's
Possess on.					
Thing.	7. io something anything	16. ĉio everything all things	25. kio what (thing)	34. nenio nothing	43. tio that (thing)
Quantity.	8. iom somewhat some quantity (a little)	17. ĉiom all of it the whole	26. kiom how much how many what quantity	35. neniom none at all none no quantity	44. tiom so much } as } many
Individuality.	9. iu some } any } one	18. ĉiu each one all everyone	27. kiu who which that (rel. pronoun)	36. neniu nobody no one	45. tiu that one the former

As will be noticed from a careful reading of this list, the last four columns are formed by adding certain letters to those in first column. Speaking generally, these prefixed letters have a definite signification.

Thus, Ĉ prefixed, conveys a collective force.

K, prefixed, gives the word an interrogative or relative meaning.

T, prefixed, gives the word a demonstrative signification.

Nen, prefixed, denotes negation.

See page 81 or exercises on these words.

HOW TO BUILD UP NEW WORDS.

In order to create new words, as mentioned on pages 25 and 26, it is only necessary for the student to learn the following simple rules :—

(1). GRAMMATICAL TERMINATIONS.—For example, from the root *am'* (which expresses the idea of love), we can form

> *am'i* to love (vb.), *am'o* love (subst.), *am'a* loving (adj.), *am'e* lovingly (adv.), *mi am'as* I love, etc., etc.
>
> *mort'* (the idea of death), *mort'i* to die, *mort'o* death, *mort'a* mortal (adj.), *mort'int'o* (the) deceased, etc.
>
> *parol'i* to speak, *parol'o* speech, *parol'a* oral, spoken, *parol'ant'o* speaker, etc.
>
> *natur'o* nature, *natur'a* natural, *nature*, naturally, etc.

(2) PREFIXES AND SUFFIXES (of which some thirty are in common use) ·

mal—denotes the opposite of any idea:

> *bon'a* good, *mal'bon'a* evil ;
> *amik'o* friend, *mal'amik'o* enemy.
> *fort'a* strong, *mal'fort'a* weak ;
> *bel'a* beautiful, *mal'bel'a* ugly ;
> *ĝoj'i* to rejoice, *mal'ĝoj'i* to mourn ;
> *ben'i* to bless, *mal'ben'i* to curse.

in—denotes the feminine gender :

> *patr'o* father, *patr'in'o* mother ;
> *frat'o* brother, *frat'in'o* sister ;
> *knab'o* boy, *knab'in'o* girl ;
> *bov'o* bull, *bov'in'o* cow.

il—denotes the instrument by which something is done :

tranĉi to cut, *tranĉil'o* a knife ;
komb'i to comb, *komb'il'o* comb ;
kudr'i to sew, *kudr'il'o* needle ;
tond'i to clip, *tond'il'o* scissors.

ad—denotes the continuation of an action ·

spir'i to breathe, *spir'ad'o* respiration, breathing ;
puŝ'o a push, *puŝ'ad'o* a pushing ;
instru'i to instruct, *instru'ad'o* instruction.

aĵ—denotes something made from, or having the quality of what is mentioned :

mal'nov'a old, *mal'nov'aĵ'o* an old thing, an antique ;
mol'a soft, *mol'aĵ'o* a soft thing ;
frit'i to fry, *frit'aĵ'o* a fritter.

an—denotes a member, inhabitant, or partisan :

ŝtat'o a state, *ŝtat'an'o* a member of a state, a citizen ;
vilaĝ'o a village, *vilaĝ'an'o* a villager ;
Amerik'o America, *Amerik'an'o* an American.

ar—denotes a collection of the thing mentioned :

arb'o a tree, *arb'ar'o* a forest ;
insul'o an island, *insul'ar'o* an archipelago ;
vort'o a word, *vort'ar'o* a dictionary.

bo—denotes a relative by marriage :

patr'o father, *bo'patr'o* father-in-law ;
fil'o son, *bo'fil'o* son-in-law.

ĉj—these letters added to the first few letters of a masculine name make of it an affectionate diminutive:

Petr'o Peter, *Pe'ĉj'o* Pete ;

for feminine names add *nj* instead of *ĉj* :

Helen'o Helen, *Hele'nj'o, He'nj'o,* Nellie.

dis—denotes separation and dissemination :
    ĵet'i to throw, *dis'ĵet'i* to throw about ;
    sem'i to sow, *dis'sem'i* to scatter, disseminate.

ebl—denotes possibility :
    kred'i to believe, *kred'ebl'a* credible ;
    fleks'i to bend, *fleks'ebl'a* flexible ;
    leg'i to read, *leg'ebl'a* legible.

ec—denotes an abstract quality :
    bel'a beautiful, *bel'ec'o* beauty ;
    vir'in'o woman, *vir'in'ec'o* womanliness ;
    amik'o friend, *amik'ec'o* friendliness ;
    simpl'a simple, *simpl'ec'o* simplicity.

edz—denotes a married person
    doktor'o doctor, *doktor'edz'in'o* doctor's wife.

eg—denotes enlargement or intensity of degree :
    pord'o door, *pord'eg'o* portal, outer-door ;
    varm'a warm, *varm'eg'a* hot ;
    bru'o a noise, *bru'eg'o* a tumult ;
    paf'il'o gun, *paf'il'eg'o* cannon.

ej—denotes the place where the action indicated by
    the root word takes place :
    dorm'i to sleep, *dorm'ej'o* a dormitory ;
    preĝ'i to pray, *preĝ'ej'o* church ;
    lern'i to learn, *lern'ej'o* school.

ek—denotes an action which begins or is of short
    duration :
    kant'i to sing, *ek'kant'i* to begin to sing ;
    dorm'i to sleep, *ek'dorm'i* to fall asleep ;
    rid'i to laugh, *ek'rid'i* to burst out laughing.

em—denotes propensity or disposition :
    envi'i to envy, *envi'em'a* envious ;
    kred'i to believe, *kred'em'a* credulous ;
    ŝpar'i to be sparing, *ŝpar'em'a* frugal.

er—denotes one object of a collection :
  sabl'o sand, *sab'ler'o* a grain of sand ;
  polv'o dust, *polv'er'o* a grain of dust ;
  mon'o money, *mon'er'o* a coin ;
  hajl'o hail, *hajl'er'o* a hailstone.

estr—denotes a chief, leader, or ruler :
  šip'o ship, *šip'estr'o* captain ;
  regn'o kingdom, *regn'estr'o* ruler.

et—denotes diminution of degree :
  bird'o a bird, *bird'et'o* a little bird ;
  rid'i to laugh, *rid'et'i* to smile ;
  dorm'i to sleep, *dorm'et'i* to doze ;
  mal'varm'a cold, *mal'varm'et'a* cool.

ge—denotes persons of both sexes, taken together ·
  patr'o father, *ge'patr'o'j* parents ;
  mastr'o master, *ge'mastr'o'j* master and mistress ;
  edz'o husband, *ge'edz'o'j* married pair.

id—denotes a child or descendant, or the young of :
  kat'o cat, *kat'id'o* kitten ;
  Napoleon'o Napoleon, *Napoleon'id'o* descendant of
    Napoleon ;
  bov'o ox, *bov'id'o* calf ;
  šaf'o sheep, *šaf'id'o* lamb.

ig – denotes the causing anything to be (in a certain
    state) :
  mort'i to die, *mort'ig'i* to kill ;
  bel'a beautiful, *bel'ig'i* to beautify ;
  pli'grand'a larger, *pli'grand'ig'i* to enlarge.

iĝ—denotes the action of becoming, turning to :
  riĉ'a rich, *riĉ'iĝ'i* to enrich one's self ;
  ruĝ'a red, *ruĝ'iĝ'i* to blush ;
  al to, *al'iĝ'i* to join one's self to.

ind—denotes worthiness :
  kred'i to believe, *kred'ind'a* worthy of belief
  laŭd'i to praise, *laŭd'ind'a* praiseworthy ;
  estim'i to esteem, *estim'ind'a* estimable.

ing—denotes a holder, that into which one object is
    appropriately put :
  cigar'o cigar, *cigar'ing'o* a cigar-holder ;
  kandel'o a candle, *kandel'ing'o* a candlestick ;
  plum'o a pen, *plum'ing'o* a penholder.

ist—denotes a person of a given profession or
    occupation :
  drog'o a drug, *drog'ist'o* a druggist ;
  ŝtel'i to steal, *ŝtel'ist'o* thief ;
  lav'i to wash, *lav'ist'in'o* washerwoman
  bot'o boot, *bot'ist'o* bootmaker.

moŝt'o—a general title of politeness :
  reg'o king, *li'a reg'a moŝt'o* his majesty ;
  princ'o prince, *Vi'a princ'a moŝt'o* your royal highness ;
  Vi'a moŝt'o your honour, your worship.

re—corresponds to the English *re* = again, back :
  kon'i to know, *re'kon'i* to recognise ;
  don'i to give, *re'don'i* to give back.

uj—denotes that which bears, contains, or produces :
  ink'o ink, *ink'uj'o* an inkstand ;
  mon'o money, *mon'uj'o* purse ;
  plum'o pen, *plum'uj'o* pen-case ;
  pom'o apple, *pom'uj'o* apple-tree ;
  Turk'o a Turk, *Turk'uj'o* Turkey.

ul—denotes one remarkable for a given quality ·
  bel'a beauty, *bel'ul'in'o* a beauty (feminine)
  tim'o fear, *tim'ul'o* a coward ;
  riĉ'a rich, *riĉ'ul'o* a rich person.

PART II.—EXERCISES ON THE GRAMMAR.

VOCABULARY FOR LESSONS 1 & 2.

Mal, Prefix, denotes contraries, as *Amiko*, Friend
Malamiko, Enemy.

As (final), denotes present tense of verbs. *Is* (final),
denotes past tense.

Patro,	Father.	*Li*,	He.
Frato,	Brother.	*Ŝi*,	She.
Knabo,	Boy.	*Trovi*,	To find
Hundo,	Dog.	*Libro*,	Book.
Riĉa,	Rich.	*Rozo*,	Rose.
Sana,	Healthy.	*Sur*,	Upon, on.
Forta,	Strong.	*Tablo*,	Table.
Amiko,	Friend.	*Vidi*,	To see.
Kaj,	And.	*Granda*,	Great.
La,	The.	*En*,	In, into.
Ĝi,	It.	*Ĝardeno*,	Garden.
Jen estas, { Here is.		*Esti*,	To be.
Here are.		*Ĉambro*,	Chamber.
Pomo,	Apple.	*Kun*,	With.
Floro,	Flower.	*Ĉielo*,	Sky.
Birdo,	Bird.	*Blua*,	Blue.
Tre,	Very.	*Multe*,	Many, much.
Bona,	Good.	*Da*,	Of.
Sed,	But.	*De*,	Of.
Filo,	Son.	*Domo*,	House.
Mi,	I.	*Onklo*,	Uncle.
Havi,	To have.	*Bela*,	Beautiful.

* Used only after words indicating—Quantity, Weight,
Measure, Number.

D

LESSON 1.—TRANSLATION.

(To be read aloud and translated by Student).

Patro, patrino.   Frato, fratino.   Knabo, knabino,
Hundo, hundino.   Riĉa, malriĉa.   Sana, malsana.
Forta, malforta.   Amiko, malamiko.   Patro kaj
patrino.   La frato kaj la fratino.   Jen estas la pomo,
la floro, la birdo kaj la libro.   La patro estas tre bona
sed la filo estas malbona.   Mi havas la floron.   Ŝi
havas pomojn.   Mi trovis bonan libron.   La rozoj
estas sur la tablo.   Mi vidis grandan hundon en la
ĝardeno.   Li estas en la ĉambro kun la onklino.   La
ĉielo estas blua.   La patroj kaj la patrinoj havas
multe da libroj kaj birdoj.   La onkloj estas tre
malriĉaj.   La domo de la onklino estas tre bela.   Jen
estas la libro.

LESSON 2.—COMPOSITION.

The father and the mother.   I have a rose.   The
fathers are in the chamber.   The daughter is very
good.   The uncle is poor.   The dog is weak.   Here
is the beautiful book.   He is an enemy.   The uncle is
a very good friend.   A rose and a book are on the
table.   The uncles and the aunts have a very beautiful
house and garden.   She is in the chamber with the
dog of the aunt.   I am strong but he is very weak.
I found good books on the table in the room.   Good
books are good friends, but bad books are enemies.
She saw beautiful birds in the small garden.   The
girls are very good but the boys are bad.   He found
many books.

VOCABULARY FOR LESSONS 3 & 4.

Eg, Augmentative, denoting highest degree, as
Bruo, A noise, *Bruego*, A tumult, An uproar. *Varmega*,
Broiling hot.

Et, Diminutive, denoting decrease, as *Birdo*, A bird. *Birdeto*, A little bird.

Varma,	Warm.	*Tie,*	There (place).
Pluvo,	Rain.	*Kio,*	What (thing)
Pordo,	Door.	*Voli,*	To wish.
Arbo,	Tree.	*Bela,*	Beautiful.
Dormi,	To sleep.	*Ĉevalo,*	Horse.
Blanka,	White.	*Doni,*	To give.
Papero,	Paper.	*Al,*	To.
Juna,	Young.	*Paroli,*	To speak.
Filo,	Son.	*Fumi,*	To smoke.
Fluanta,	Flowing.	*Cigaro,*	Cigar.
Akvo,	Water.	*Sinjoro,*	Sir.
Amanta,	Loving.	*Jes,*	Yes.
Feliĉa,	Happy.	*Ofte,*	Often.
Os marks the future		*Hodiaŭ,*	To-day.
tense.		*Pri,*	About. Concerning.
Aĉeti,	To buy.		
Teo,	Tea.	*Hieraŭ,*	Yesterday.
Kafo,	Coffee.	*Bezoni,*	To need, want.
Kremo,	Cream.	*Legi,*	To read.
Sukero,	Sugar.	*Morgaŭ,*	To-morrow.
Trinki,	To drink.	*Tiu ĉi,*	This.
Kiu,	Who, which.	*Tago,*	Day.
Frapi,	To knock.		

LESSON 3.—TRANSLATION.

Varma, varmega. Granda, grandega. Pluvo, pluvego. Pordo, pordego. Libro, libreto. Domo, dometo. Arbo, arbeto. Varma, varmeta. Dormi, dormeti. Blanka papero. Blankaj paperoj. Juna filo. Junaj filoj. Fluanta akvo. Amantaj amikoj. Feliĉa knabo. Feliĉaj knabinoj. Mi aĉetos teon, kafon, kremon kaj sukeron. Ĉu* vi trinkos akvon,

---

* Ĉu denotes an interrogation when no other interrogative word such as Kiu, Kio, Kia, etc., is used.

vinon aŭ teon? Kiu frapas? Kiu estas tie? Kiu vi estas? Kion vi volas? Mi volas vidi la belan ĉevaleton! Donu al mi la libreton. Mi parolos al la patro. Ĉu vi fumas, sinjoro? Jes, mi ofte fumas cigaron. Vi trovos la paperojn sur la tableto en la ĝardenego (or granda ĝardeno). Mi havas belan dometon. Mi estas juna, li estas pli juna, sed ŝi estas la plej juna. Mi parolos hodiaŭ al mia patro, pri la libro, kiun vi donis al mi hieraŭ. Mi bezonas paroli kun vi. Mi legos morgaŭ tiun ĉi libron. Bonan tagon, sinjorino.

LESSON 4.—COMPOSITION.

Father, mother. Brother, sister. Boy, girl. Dog (m.), bitch. Rich, poor. Healthy, unhealthy. Strong, weak. Friend, enemy. Father and mother. The brother and the sister. Here is the apple, the flower, the bird and the book. The father is very good, but the son is bad. I have the flower. She has apples. I found (or have found) a good book. The roses are on the table. I saw a great dog in the garden. He is in the room with the aunt. The sky is blue. The fathers and the mothers have many books and birds. The uncles are very poor. The aunt's house is very beautiful. Here is the book.

VOCABULARY FOR LESSONS 5 & 6.

Ec, Suffix, denotes a quality (abstract). *Feliĉa,* Happy. *Feliĉeco,* Happiness.

Ar, Suffix, denotes a collection of things mentioned. *Insulo,* An island. *Insularo,* An archipelago. *Arbo,* A tree. *Arbaro,* A forest.

Simpla,	Simple.	*Vorto,*	Word.
Ebria,	Drunk.	*Sana,*	Healthy.
Vagono,	{ Wagon. Carriage.	*Kontenta,*	{ Contented. Pleased.
Branĉo,	Branch (tree).	*Ke,*	That (conjn.).

Povi,	To be able.	*Longa,*	Long.
Esti,	To be.	*Larĝa,*	Wide.
Utila,	Useful.	*El,*	{ Out of.
Prezenti,	To present.		{ Amongst.
Konsili,	{ To advise.	*Ĉiuj,*	All.
	{ Counsel.	*Min,*	Me (obj.).
Fari,	To do, make.	*Koni,*	To know.
Ne,	No, not.	*Honoro,*	Honor.
Scii,	To know.	*Vin,*	You (obj.).
E denotes adverbs.		*Proksima,*	Near, next.
Bone,	Well.	*Mia,*	{ My, mine
Ĝi,	It.		{ (poss.).
Afero,	{ Affair, Matter	*Saluto*	Salutation.
	{ Cause.	*Saĝa,*	Wise.
Grava,	Important.	*Vetero*	Weather.
Pano,	Bread.	*Kara,*	Dear.
Freŝa,	Fresh, New.	*Ricevi,*	To receive.
Tiu,	{ That (demv.	*Via,*	Your (poss.).
	{ adj.) or that	*Ĉarma,*	Charming.
	{ person.	*Poŝta Karto*	} Post Card.
Sincera,	Sincere.	or*Poŝtkarto,*	}
Admiri,	To admire.	*Letero,*	Letter.
Tuj	{ At once.	*Respondi,*	To answer.
	{ Immediately.	*Danki,*	To thank.

LESSON 5.—TRANSLATION.

Simpla, simpleco. Bela, beleco. Ebria, ebrieco. Amiko, amikeco. Vagono, vagonaro. Branĉo, branĉaro. Vorto, vortaro. Arbo, arbaro. Kio estas pli bona ol saneco? Mi estas tre kontenta, ke mi povis esti utila al vi. Kion vi konsilas al mi fari? Mi ne scias bone; ĝi estas afero grava. Tiu ĉi pano estas freŝa, sed tiu estas pli freŝa. Li admiris la longecon kaj la larĝecon de tiu ĉi arbaro. Mi havas la plej grandan vortaron el ĉiuj. Ĉu vi min konas?

Mi ne havas la honoron vin koni. Li estas proksima,
ŝi estas pli proksima, sed Johano estas la plej
proksima el ĉiuj. El ĉiuj miaj amikoj, Ernesto estas
la malplej forta. Ili estas tre feliĉaj. Ŝi estas tiel
saĝa kiel bela. Ĉu estas malvarma vetero hodiaŭ?
Jes, hodiaŭ estas bela vetero. Kara Sinjoro, Mi
ricevis vian ĉarman poŝtkarton kaj leteron, al kiuj
mi tuj respondas. Mi dankas vin, kaj prezentas al
vi miajn sincerajn salutojn.

LESSON 6.—COMPOSITION.

Warm, intensely warm. Great, huge. Rain, a
downpour. Door, gate (portal). Book, booklet
(tract). House, cottage (little house). Tree, shrub.
Warm, cool, lukewarm. To sleep, to doze. White
paper, white papers. A young son. Young sons.
Flowing water. Loving friends. A happy boy.
Happy girls. I shall buy tea, coffee, cream and sugar.
Will you drink water, wine or tea? Who knocks
Who is there? Who are you? What do you want?
I wish to see the beautiful little horse. Give (to)
me the little book (booklet). I shall speak to the
father. Do you smoke, Sir? Yes, I often smoke a
cigar. You will find the papers on the little table in
the immense garden. I have a beautiful cottage. I
am young, he is younger, but she is the youngest.
I shall speak to-day to my father about (concerning)
the book which you gave (to) me yesterday. I need
to speak with you. I shall read this book to-morrow.
Good day, Madam.

VOCABULARY FOR LESSONS 7 & 8.

Ek, Prefix, denotes an action which begins, or is of
short duration. *Brili*, To shine. *Ekbrili*, To flash.

Il, Suffix, denotes the instrument by which a thing is done. *Kombi*, To comb. *Kombilo*, A comb.

Ridi,	To laugh.	*Mardo,*	Tuesday.
Kanti,	To sing.	*Jaŭdo,*	Thursday.
Krii,	To cry (out).	*Februaro,*	February.
Bori,	To bore.	*Monato,*	Month.
Ĉizi,	To carve (with a chisel)	*Jaro,*	Year.
		Aprilo,	April.
Gladi,	To iron.	*Aŭgusto,*	August.
Filtri,	To filter.	*Oktobro,*	October.
Okulo,	Eye.	*Novembro,*	November.
Orelo,	Ear.	*Pensi,*	To think.
Mano,	Hand.	*Se,*	If.
Buŝo,	Mouth.	*Nur,*	Only.
Ili,	They.	*Iri,*	To go.
Promeni,	To promenade.	*Teatro,*	Theatre.
		Skribi,	To write.
Ĉiutage,	Every day.	*Kelke (da),*	Some (of).
Kampo,	Field.	*Sendi,*	To send.
Ĝentila,	{ Polite. Gentle.	*Alportanto,*	A bearer.
Ol,	Than.	*Zorgi,*	{ To care about. To see to.
Dimanĉo,	Sunday.	*Bileto,*	Ticket.
Semajno,	Week.	*Kore,*	Heartily.

Os final denotes the future tense.
I final denotes the infinitive mood.

LESSON 7.—TRANSLATION.

Ridi, ekridi. Dormi, ekdormj. Kanti, ekkanti. Krii, ekkrii. Bori, borilo. Ĉizi, ĉizilo. Gladi, gladilo. Filtri, filtrilo. Mi havas du okulojn, du orelojn, du manojn, sed mi havas nur unu buŝon. Ili promenas ĉiutage en la kampo kun du grandaj hundoj. Dek kaj dudek faras tridek. Kvardek-unu kaj dek-naŭ faras sesdek. Kvin homoj povas fari pli multe ol unu. Dimanĉo estas la unua tago de la semajno, mardo estas la tria kaj ĵaŭdo estas la kvina. Februaro estas la plej mallonga monato de la jaro, ĉar ĝi havas nur dudek-ok tagojn. Aprilo estas la kvara monato de la jaro, Aŭgusto estas la oka, Oktobro estas la deka kaj Novembro estas la dek-unua. Kara sinjoro; kion vi pensas, se hodiaŭ ni irus en la teatron? Skribu kelkajn vortojn de respondo kaj sendu ilin per la alportanto de tiu ĉi letero. Mi zorgos pri la biletoj. Kore mi vin salutas.

LESSON 8.—COMPOSITION.

Simple, simplicity. Beautiful, beauty. Drunk, drunkenness. Friend, friendliness. Wagon, car (railroad), train. Branch, faggot. Word, dictionary. Tree, forest. What is better than health? I am very pleased that I could be useful to you. What do you counsel (advise) me to do? I do not well know, it is a grave (or important) matter (affair). This bread is fresh, but that is fresher. He admired the length and breadth of this forest. I have the largest dictionary of (el) all. Do you know me? I have not the honour to know you. He is near, she is nearer, but John is the nearest of (el) all. Amongst all my friends Ernest is the least strong. They are very happy. She is as wise as beautiful. Is it cold weather to-day? Yes, to-day (it) is beautiful weather. Dear Sir, I received your charming post-card and letter, to which I reply at once (immediately). I thank you; and present (tender) to you my sincere salutations.

VOCABULARY FOR LESSONS 9 & 10.

Bo, Prefix, denotes relatives by marriage. *Patrino*, Mother. *Bopatrino*, Mother-in-law.

Ge, Prefix, persons of both sexes taken together. *Mastro*, Master. *Mastrino*, Mistress. *Gemastroj*, Master and mistress.

Edzo,	Husband.	*Kredi,*	To believe.
Mastro,	Master.	*Li,*	He.
Kordo,	String (piano, etc.)	*Kuri,*	To run.
		Ludi,	To play.
Fadeno,	Thread.	*Ĝi,*	It.
Regimento,	Regiment.	*Kreski,*	To grow.
Marŝi,	{ To march. To walk.	*Serĉi,*	To seek.
		Rimarki,	To remark.
Tra,	Through.	*Aŭskulti,*	To listen.
Strato,	Street.	*Afabla,*	Amiable.
Kapabla,	Capable.	*Avo,*	Grandfather.
Atenta,	Attentive.	*Po,*	At the rate of.
Inteligenta.	Intelligent.	*Korekte,*	Correctly.
Monto,	Mountain.	*Aminda,*	Affectionate.
Nia,	Our, ours.	*Donaco,*	Gift.
Vilaĝo,	Village.	*Ĉiu,*	Each, every.
Alta,	High.	*Fini,*	To finish.
Metro,	Metre.	*Rigardi,*	To look at.
Ĉeno,	Chain.	*Jurnalo,*	Newspaper.
Historio,	History.	*U* denotes	imperative
Paĝo,	Page.	mood.	
Frue,	Early.		

LESSON 9.—TRANSLATION.

Patro, bopatro. Filo, bofilo. Filino, bofilino. Fratoj, bofratoj. Edzo, edzino, geedzoj. Mastro, mastrino, gemastroj. Filo, gefiloj. Dek estas la kvin sesonoj de dek-du. Ok estas la kvinono de kvardek. Mi bezonas trioblan kordon. La unuobla fadeno ne estas tiel forta kiel la duobla fadeno La

regimento marŝis dekope tra la stratoj. Tiuj ĉi
homoj estas kapablaj, atentaj kaj inteligentaj. La
monteto en nia vilaĝo estas alta kvarcent metrojn.
Kvarobla ĉeno estas tre forta, sed sepobla ĉeno estas
pli forta. Mia historio havas sepdek-du paĝojn.
Venu duope aŭ triope, sed venu frue. Mi kredas, li
kuras, ŝi ludas, ĝi kreskas, ni serĉas, vi rimarkas, ili
aŭskultas. Mia afabla avino donis al ni po kvin
pomoj ĉar ni kantis korekte. Mia aminda avo donis
al li donacon. Se mi legos tiun ĉi libron po dek-du
paĝoj en ĉiu horo, mi ĝin finos en dek-du horoj.
Rigardu la maljunan sinjoron, kiu legas la ĵurnalon.

LESSON 10.—COMPOSITION.

To laugh, to begin to laugh. To sleep, to fall
asleep. To sing, to begin to sing. To cry, to begin
to cry, or cry out. To bore, a gimlet. To carve
(sculpture), a chisel. To iron (clothes), a flat iron.
To filter, a filter. I have two eyes, two ears, two
hands, but I have only one mouth. They promenade
(take a walk) daily in the field with two great dogs.
Ten and twenty make thirty. Forty-one and nine-
teen make sixty. Five men can do much more than
one. Sunday is the first day of the week, Tuesday
is the third, and Thursday is the fifth. February is
the shortest month of the year, because it has only
twenty-eight days. April is the fourth month of the
year, August is the eighth, October is the tenth, and
November is the eleventh. Dear Sir, What do* you
think, if we should go to-day to (en) the theatre ?
Write a few words of reply and send them by the
bearer of this letter   I will see about the tickets.
I salute you heartily.

---

* "Do" is not translated. Kion vi pensas?=What do
you think ?

VOCABULARY FOR LESSONS 11 & 12.

Ad, Suffix, denotes the continuation of an action *Spiri*, To breathe. *Spirado*, Respiration, breathing.

Ej, Suffix, denotes place generally devoted to *Lerni*, To learn. *Lernejo*, A school.

Fabriko,	Manufactory.	*Rezignacio*,	Resignation.
Gimnastika,	Gymnastic.	*Tondro*,	Thunder.
Distili,	To distil.	*Kaŭzi*,	To cause.
Vero,	Truth.	*Konfuzo*,	Confusion.
Kanto,	Song.	*Serĝento*,	Serjeant.
Bano,	Bath.	*Jeti*,	To throw.
Preferi,	To prefer.	*Inter*,	{ Between.
Lavi,	To wash.		Amongst.
Gasto,	Guest.	*Antaŭ ol*,	Before (time.)
Vespero,	Evening.	*Tempo*,	Time.
Aparteni,	To belong	*Fermi*,	To close.
Skatolo,	Box.	*Por*,	{ For.
Plumo,	Pen.		In order to.
Alia,	Other.	*Protesti*,	To protest.
Objekto,	Object.	*Meti*,	To put.
Ant, sign of	pres. part.	*Infano*,	Child.
Reveni,	To return.	*Brako*,	Arm.
Tombo,	Tomb.	*Rigardi*,	To look at.
Konsolo,	Consolation.	*Ankoraŭ*,	Again.
Vere,	Truly.	*Unu fojo*,	Once.
Morti,	To die.	*Kuri*,	To run.
Kristano,	Christian.	*For*,	Away, far off.
Mirinda,	Wonderful.	*Vojo*,	Road, way.

LESSON 11.—TRANSLATION.

Iri, irado. Fabriki, fabrikado. Instrui, Instruado. Parolo, parolado. Greno, grenejo. Dormi, dormejo. Distili, distilejo. Mi serĉos la veron. Ĉu vi aŭdas la kantojn de miaj birdoj? Ŝi estas nia malamiko (or, malamikino). Vi lavos vin en via banejo, sed li preferas sin lavi en la dormoĉambro. Liaj filoj havos gastojn hodiaŭ vespere. Tiu ĉi libro apartenas al mia patrino. En via skatoleto estas plumoj kaj aliaj objektoj. " Mia kara amiko," li diris al mi, revenante el la tombejo, " vi havas konsolon en via malfeliĉo. Via filino vere mortis kristane kaj kun mirinda rezignacio." Se tondro falus sur nin, ĝi ne povus kaŭzi pli grandan konfuzon ol la unua vorto kiun serĝento Ĉermak jetis inter nin. Antaŭ ol li havis la tempon malfermi la buŝon por protesti, ŝi metis la infaneton sur liajn brakojn, rigardis lin ankoraŭ unu fojon kaj forkuris rapide tra la vojo.

LESSON 12.—COMPOSITION.

Father, father-in-law. Son, son-in-law. Daughter, daughter-in-law. Brothers, brothers-in-law. Husband, wife, husband " and " wife. Master, mistress, master "and" mistress. Son, son " and " daughter. Ten is the five sixths of twelve. Eight is the fifth of forty. I need a triple cord. The single thread is not as (or so) strong as the double thread. The regiment marched by tens through the streets. These men are capable, attentive and intelligent. The hill in our village is 400 metres high. A fourfold chain is very strong, but a sevenfold chain is stronger. My history (book) has 72 pages. Come two together or three together, but come early. I believe, he runs, she plays, it grows, we seek, you remark, they listen. My affable grandmother gave us each (po) 5 apples because we sang correctly. My affectionate grandfather gave him a gift (a present). If I shall read this book at the rate of 12 pages in each hour, I shall finish it in 12 hours. Look at the old gentleman who reads (or is reading) the newspaper.

VOCABULARY FOR LESSONS 13 & 14.

Aj, Suffix, denotes something possessing a certain quality, or something made from a certain substance, a thing perceptible to the senses. It differs from the Suffix *ec*, in this,.that *aj* conveys a concrete idea, and *ec* an abstract idea. *Pentri*, To paint. *Pentrajo*, A painting. *Bona*, Good. *Bonajo*, A good thing. *Malbonajo*, A bad thing.

Re, Prefix, denotes a repetition of an act, or a return to something, to do again. It has, generally, the same meaning as the English Prefix *re*. *Iri*, To go. *Reiri*, To go again. *Doni*, To give. *Redoni*, To give back. *Veni*, To arrive. *Reveni*, To return.

Mola,	Soft.	*Servanto*,	Servant.
Frukto,	Fruit.	*Retiri*,	To withdraw.
Heroo,	Hero.	*Seĝo*,	Chair.
Friti,	To fry.	*Estingi*,	To extinguish
Frandulo,	Epicure.	*Kandelo*,	Candle.
Komenci,	To commence	*Kutimo*,	{ Custom. Habit.
Produkti,	To produce.		
Diri,	To say.	*Ĉapitro*	Chapter.
Aperi,	To appear.	*Biblio*,	Bible.
Brili,	To shine.	*Restajo*,	{ Rest (noun). Remains.
Voki,	To call.		
Fianĉo,	{ Sweetheart (mas.). Betrothed (mas.).	*Kuko*,	Cake.
		Kukajo,	Pastry.
		Peni,	To endeavour
		Okupi,	To occupy.
Veni,	To come.	*Profunde*,	{ Deeply. Profoundly.
Virino,	Woman.		
Vilaĝano,	Villager.	*Desegno*,	{ Design, drawing.
Nepo,	Grandson.		
Aĝo,	Age.	*Posedi*,	To possess.
Renkonti,	To meet.	*Arto*,	Art.
Nevo,	Nephew.	*Konformi*,	To conform.
Tolo,	Linen.	*Ĝuste*,	Exactly.
Estimata,	Esteemed.	*Maniero*,	Manner.
Tuta,	All.	*Sekso*,	Sex.
Respekto,	Respect.	*Pozicio*,	Position.
Humila,	Humble.	*Persono*,	Person.

LESSON 13.—TRANSLATION.

Mola, molaĵo. Blanka, blankaĵo. Frukto, fruktaĵo
Amiko, amikaĵo. Heroo, heroaĵo. Sukero, sukeraĵo.
Friti, fritaĵo. Frando, frandaĵo. Komenci, rekomenci
Koni, rekoni. Produkti, reprodukti. Diri, rediri.
Ĵeti, reĵeti. Aperi, reaperi. Brili, rebrili. Voki,
revoki. La fratino de la mastro kuris al sia fianĉo.
Tiu ĉi sinjoro venos al mi morgaŭ por ke mi redonu
liajn librojn al li. La avo malamas tiun ĉi virinon,
sed li amas ŝian filon. La ĉevalo konas sian mastron
kaj ĝi kuras al li. Kiu estas en la ĝardeno ? La
vilaĝano estas en la ĝardeno kun sia nepo. Kiun
aĝon vi havas ? Ernesto renkontis sian nevon kaj
siajn amikojn. Ernesto renkontis sian nevon kaj liajn
amikojn. Kie estas la tolaĵo? La tolaĵo estas en la
banejo. Mi esperas, estimata sinjorino, ke vi skribos al
mi tre baldaŭ pri tiu ĉi afero, kaj mi restas kun tuta
respekto via plej humila servanto. Li retiris de mi
la seĝon. Li estingis la kandelon, sed li ne povis, laŭ sia
kutimo, legi ĉapitron el sia Biblio. Mi donis al li la
restaĵon de tiu kuko. Mi nenion respondis kaj penis
min okupi profunde per miaj desegnoj. Sinjoro Nolasco
posedis la arton konformigi ĝuste siajn parolojn kaj
manierojn al la aĝo, la sekso kaj la pozicio de la
personoj kun kiuj li parolis.

LESSON 14.—COMPOSITION.

To go, a going, a movement (as of machinery).
To manufacture, manufacturing. To instruct (to
teach), instruction (n.). A word (spoken not
written), a speech or discourse. Grain (corn), granary.
To sleep, dormitory. To distil, distillery. I will
seek the truth Do you hear the songs of my
birds ? She is our enemy. You will wash yourself
in your bath (room), but he prefers to wash himself
in the bedroom. His sons will have guests (com-
pany) this (to-day) evening. This book belongs to

my mother. In your little box are pens and other objects. "My dear friend," he said to me, on returning from the cemetery, "you have (the) consolation in your unhappiness. Your daughter truly died Christianly (in a Christian manner) and with wonderful resignation." If a thunder (bolt) should fall upon us, it could not cause greater confusion than the first word which Sergeant Chermak threw amongst us. Before he had (the) time to open his (the) mouth (in order) to protest, she put the little infant into his arms, looked at him once (one time) again and ran away rapidly across the road.

VOCABULARY FOR LESSONS 15 & 16.

Ig, Suffix, denotes "to make," "to render." *Densa*, Dense. *Densigi*, To make dense, to condense. *Perfekta*, Perfect. *Perfektigi*, To make, or render, perfect.

Iĝ, Suffix, denotes "to become." In some cases this suffix gives a reflexive force to the verb. *Certa*, Sure, certain. *Certiĝi*, To become certain. *Riĉa*, Rich. *Riĉiĝi*, To become rich, to enrich one's self. *Granda*, Big, large. *Grandiĝi*, To become big, tall.

Forta,	Strong.	*Grasa,*	{ Stout. { Fat.
*Klara,	{ Distinct. { Clear.	*Peti*	To beg.
Grupo,	Group.	*Petegi,*	To beseech.
Nobla,	Noble.	*Sidiĝi,*	To be seated.
Matura,	{ Mature. { Ripe.	*Fenestro,*	Window.
		Loko,	Place.
Pala,	Pale.	*Dante',*	Dante.
Ruĝa,	Red.	*Prava,*	{ Right. { Just.
Hela,	{ Bright. { Clear.	*Infero,*	Hell.

---

* Clear ; not confused, mentally clear

Pavimi,	To pave.	*Neniam,*	Never.
Intenco,	Intention.	*Samtempe,*	At once.
Kioma,	{ What (adj)?	*Ĉio,*	Everything.
	{ Which ?	*Proverbo,*	Proverb.
Kuŝiĝi,	{ To go to bed.	*Plezuro,*	Pleasure.
	{ To rest.	*Vespermanĝi,*	To dine.
Somero,	Summer.	*Bedaŭri,*	{ To regret (to
Vintro,	Winter.		{ be sorry).
Sekvi,	To follow.	*Akcepti,*	To accept.
Ekzemplo,	Example.	*Invito,*	Invitation.
Devi,	{ To be	*Malsaneto,*	{ A slight
	{ obliged to.		{ indisposition
Principo,	Principle.		

LESSON 15.—TRANSLATION.

Bela, Beligi. Forta, Fortigi. Klara, Klarigi.
Morti, Mortigi. Grupo, Grupigi. Nobla, Nobligi.
Longa, Longigi. Mola, Moligi. Matura, Maturiĝi.
Pala, Paliĝi. Ruĝa, Ruĝiĝi. Hela, Heliĝi. Maljuna,
Maljuniĝi. Varma, Varmiĝi. Grasa, Grasiĝi.
Sinjorinoj, mi petas sidiĝi. Ne metu min tiel
proksime de la fenestro, mi preferas lokon proksime
de la pordo. Dante' estis prava dirante ke la Infero
estas pavimita per bonaj intencoj. Je* kioma† horo
vi kuŝiĝas ? Je la deka horo en la somero kaj en la
vintro. Mia kara amiko, mi penos sekvi vian
ekzemplon. Mi devas diri al vi antaŭe (or antaŭ ĉio),
ke mi havas la principon neniam fari du aferojn
samtempe. Estas tempo por ĉio, diras la proverbo.
Morgaŭ vespere ni estos en la domo kaj vi faros al ni
grandan plezuron, se vi venos je la horo kutima por
vespermanĝi kun ni. Mi multe bedaŭras, ke mi ne

---

* This preposition is used, in all cases, where there is any
difficulty in finding another suitable one.

† *Kioma.* This interrogative is used when asking questions relating to time, hours, days, months, years, ordinal
numbers, pages (of a book), etc., etc.

povos akcepti la amindan inviton de vi kaj de via estimata edzino, ĉar malsaneto min retenas en mia ĉambro.

LESSON 16.—COMPOSITION.

Soft, soft substance. White, something white. Fruit, something made from fruit (such as jam). Friend, a friendly action (a kindness). Hero, an heroic act. Sugar, something made from sugar (a sweet). To fry, something fried (fritters). An epicure, a delicacy. To commence, to recommence. To know, to recognise. To produce, to reproduce. To say, to say again (to repeat). To throw, to throw back (to reject). To appear, to reappear. To shine, to reflect (to shine back again). To call, to recall. The master's sister ran to her sweetheart This gentleman will come to me to-morrow (in order) that I may return his books to him. The grandfather hates this woman, but he loves her son. The horse knows his master and he (it) runs to him. Who is in the garden ? The villager is in the garden with his grandson. How old are you ? (what age have you). Ernest met his nephew and his (Ernest's) friends. Ernest met his nephew and his (the nephew's) friends Where is the linen ? The linen is in the bath (room) I hope, esteemed Madam, that you will write to me very soon concerning this affair, and I remain with all respect your most humble servant. He withdrew the chair from me. He extinguished the candle, but he could not, according to his custom, read a chapter (out) of his Bible. I gave (to) him the remainder of that pastry (cake). I answered nothing, and tried to occupy myself profoundly with my drawings (designs). Mr. Nolasco possessed the art of exactly conforming his words and manners to the age, the sex, and the position of the persons with whom he spoke.

VOCABULARY FOR LESSONS 17 & 18.

Mono,	Money.	*Preta,*	Ready.
Olivo,	Olive.	*Atendi,*	To wait.
Almozo,	Alms.	*Denove,*	Over again.
Krimo,	Crime.		Again.
Flui,	To flow.		Thus.
Bojo,	Bark (dog's).	*Tiamaniere,*	In this man-
Muso,	Mouse.		ner.
Vidi,	To see.	*Trankvila,*	Tranquil.
Kviete,	Quietly.	*Estingi,*	To ex-
Kompreni	To under-		tinguish.
	stand.	*Palpebro,*	Eyelid.
Eĉ,	Even.	*Ankoraŭ,*	Yet still.
Adresito,	Person	*Re,*	(see prefixes,
	addressed.		etc.).
Ankaŭ,	Also	*Vizaĝo,*	Face, counte-
Sole,	Only.		nance.
Scii,	To know.	*Bukla,*	Curly (of hair)
Aldoni,	To add.	*Bruna,*	Brown.
Folio,	Leaf.	*Barbo,*	Beard.
Nomo,	Name.	*Post,*	After, behind.
Respondi,	To reply.	*Okulvitroj,*	Spectacles.
	To answer.	*Kaŝi,*	To hide.
Propono,	Proposal.	*Kuseno,*	Pillow.
Servi,	To serve.	*Ĝis,*	Until.

Antaŭ kelkaj tagoj, A few days ago, some days ago.
Iom post iom, Little by little.
Fine, Finally, lastly, at last.

LESSON 17.—TRANSLATION.

Mono, monujo. Arabo, Arabujo. Ruso, Rusujo. Kremo, Kremujo. Inko, inkujo. Pomo, pomujo (or pomarbo). Olivo, olivujo (or olivarbo). Plumo, plumingo. Kandelo, kandelingo. Pipo, pipujo. Luna, junulo. Bela, belulino. Almozo, almozulo.

Feliĉa, feliĉulo. Krimo, krimulo. Amanta patro. Fluanta rivero. Ridanta virino. Bojantaj hundoj. Muso trakuris sur korpo de dormanta leono. Vidante sian patrinon, li ekridis. Ferminte la fenestron, li dormis kviete. Mi legis antaŭ kelkaj tagoj libreton sub la titolo "Lingvo Internacia." La aŭtoro kredas, ke per tiu ĉi lingvo oni povas esti komprenata de la tuta mondo, se eĉ la adresito ne sole ne scias la lingvon, sed eĉ ankaŭ ne aŭdis pri ĝi. Oni devas sole aldoni al la letero malgrandan folieton nomatan "Vortareto." Respondante al via estimata letero ni dankas vin por via propono kaj ni plezure akceptos viajn servojn. Johano, ĉu estas preta la matenmanĝo ? Jes, Sinjoro, kaj ĝi vin atendas sur la tablo. Ŝi denove ekbruligis la lampon, kaj legis ankoraŭ ĉapitron el sia Biblio. Tiamaniere ŝi trankviliĝis iom post iom, kaj ŝi estingis la lampon. Sed ferminte la palpebrojn, ŝi ankoraŭ revidis la saman vizaĝon kun bruna bukla barbo kaj brunaj okuloj post la okulvitroj. Tiam ŝi kaŝis sian kapon en la kusenoj kaj ploris, ĝis ŝi fine ekdormis.

LESSON 18.—COMPOSITION.

Beautiful, to beautify. Strong, to strengthen. Clear (evident), to make clear (to explain). To die, to kill. Group, to group (or to form a group). Noble, to ennoble. Long, to lengthen. Soft, to make soft. Ripe, to become ripe. Pale, to become pale. Red, to blush. Bright, to become bright. Old (of a living thing), to age. Warm, to grow warm. Fat, to become fat. Ladies, I pray (you) to be seated. Do not put me so near the window, I prefer a place near the door. Dante was right in saying that hell was paved with good intentions. At what hour do you (go to) rest ? At 10 o'clock in summer and winter. My dear friend, I will try to follow your example. I ought to tell you (notify you) beforehand, that I have the principle never to do two things at once. There is a time for everything, says the proverb. To-morrow evening we shall be at home, and you will do (give) us great pleasure, if you will come at the usual hour to dine with us. I much regret that I shall not be able to accept the affectionate (kind) invitation of you and your esteemed wife, for a slight indisposition keeps me in my room.

VOCABULARY FOR LESSONS 19 & 20.

Ricevi,	To receive.	*Ist*	(see prefixes, etc.).
Vero,	Truth.		
Pastro,	Pastor. / Priest.	*Boto*	Boot.
Koni,	To know.	*Edz*	(see prefixes, etc.).
Aj	(see prefixes, etc.).	*Dis,*	(do).
		Ŝiri,	To tear.
Atingi,	To attain.	*Tiam,*	Then.
Delikata,	Gentle. / Delicate.	*Jeti,*	To throw.
		Strato,	Street.
For,	Prefix, deno- / ting "Away."	*Kolera,*	Angry.
Afabla	Affable.	*Em*	(see prefixes etc.).
Ej	(see prefixes, etc.).	*Kredi,*	To believe.
		Labori,	To labor.
Prava,	Correct. / Right, just.	*Babili,*	To prattle. / To chatter.
Tute,	All, quite.	*Livro,*	Pound (sterling).
Evidenta,	Evident.		
Kio,	What, that / which.	*Ŝilingo,*	Shilling.
		Penco,	Penny.
Rakonti,	To relate.	*Floreno,*	Florin.
Viziti,	To visit.	*Dolaro,*	Dollar.
Lavistino,	Laundress.	*Franko,*	Franc.

LESSON 19.—TRANSLATION.

Se mi estus ricevinta la libron, mi ĝin redonus. Se li amus vin, li dirus al vi la veron. Kiam ŝi estis estinta tre diligenta, la patrino laŭdis ŝin. Estas necese* ke vi estu fininta mian libron antaŭ ol mi revenos. Kiam la pastro venos, diru al li la veron. Ili ne volas doni la ĵurnalon al ni. Diru al li, ke li al mi respondu. Mi pensas ke mi venos morgaŭ. Vera amiko koniĝas en danĝero. Per amikaĵo oni ĉiam povas atingi pli multe ol per maldelikata forto. Mi foriros hodiaŭ, ĉar Johano min atendas. La sinjorino parolis afable al ni. Li staris antaŭ la pordo de la preĝejo kun amiko. La malpraveco de via parolado estis tute evidenta. Kio malplaĉos al mia patro tio malplaĉos al mi, sinjoro. La reĝido rakontis al sia patro la tutan aferon. Birdo kaptita estas pli bona ol leono kaptota. Se mi estus bona, mi estus feliĉa. Antaŭ unu monato mia onklino vizitis min. La lavistedzino vidis hieraŭ la doktored-zinon kaj la botistedzinon en la teatro. Li disŝiris la libron kaj tiam li disĵetis ĝin en la strato, ĉar li estis tre kolera. Li estas tre kredema, sed lia edzino estas mallaborema kaj babilema. Livro, ŝilingo, penco, floreno, dolaro kaj franko estas moneroj.

*When the phrase or sentence, in Esperanto, contains neither a noun nor a pronoun which an adjective in such phrase or sentence would qualify (in English), this adjective takes the adverbial termination (*e*), and not the termination of the adjective (*a*).

LESSON 20.—COMPOSITION.

Money, purse. Arab, Arabia. Russian, Russia. Cream, cream jug. Ink, ink bottle. Apple, apple tree. Olive, olive tree. Pen, penholder. Candle, candlestick. Pipe, pipe-case. Young, young man. Beautiful, beautiful woman. Alms, beggar. Happy, a happy person. Crime, criminal. A loving father. A flowing river. A laughing woman. Barking dogs. A mouse ran across (on) the body of a sleeping lion On seeing his mother he began to laugh. Having closed the window he slept quietly. I read some days ago a small book with the title of "International Language." The author believes that by means of this language one can be understood by the whole world, if even the person addressed not only does not know the language, but even, also, has not heard about it. One need only add to the letter a small leaflet, entitled "Vocabulary." Replying to your esteemed letter, we thank you for your proposal, and we will accept, with pleasure, your services. John, is (the) breakfast ready? Yes, sir, and it waits (is waiting) you on the table. She began again to light the lamp, and read again a chapter of her Bible. In this manner (thus) she became tranquil, little by little, and she extinguished the lamp. But, having closed her (the) eyelids, she still saw (again) the same face with curly-brown beard and brown eyes behind the spectacles. Then she hid her head in the pillows and wept until at last she fell asleep.

VOCABULARY FOR LESSONS 21 & 22.

Nomi,	To name.	*Beni,*	To bless.
Ŝteli,	To steal.	*Aranĝi,*	To arrange.
Pagi,	To pay.	*Bapti,*	To baptize.
Droni,	To drown.	*Bati,*	To beat.
Trompi,	To deceive.	*Kunveni,*	To assemble.
Puni,	To punish.	*Diskuti,*	To discuss.
Vesti,	{ To clothe. / To dress.	*Glaso,*	{ Glass (a vessel).
Rabi,	To pillage.	*Rompi,*	To break,
Fotografi,	{ To photograph.	*Ne-,*	Not-, un-.
		Virino,	Woman.

Ind	(see prefixes, etc.).	*Ing*	(see prefixes, etc.).
Honorinda,	Honorable.	*Uj*	do.
Lernanto,	{ Scholar, pupil.	*Poŝo,*	Pocket.
		Surtuto	Overcoat.
Fleksi,	To bend.		{ To live in.
Montri,	To show.	*Loĝi,*	{ To dwell.
Eble,	{ Probably. Possibly.		{ To inhabit.
		Anglo,	Englishman.
Helpi,	To help.	*Anglujo,*	England.
Kuiri,	To cook.	*Kuŝi,*	{ To rest on (to lie on).
Ej	(see prefixes, etc.).	*Alumeto,*	Match.
Tubo,	Tube.	*Enhavi,*	To contain.
Meti,	To put.	*Bombono,*	Bonbon.

LESSON 21.—TRANSLATION.

Mi estas amata. Vi estas nomata (sing.). Gi estas trovata. Ili estas ŝtelataj. Mi estas amita. Li estas vidita. Ni estas pagitaj. Ŝi estas dronita. Ŝi estas amota. Ili estas nomotaj. Vi estas trompotaj (pl.). Li estis punota. Mi estis nomata. Li estis vestata. Ni estis vidataj. Ili estis rabataj. Li estis amita. Vi estis fotografitaj. Ili estis benitaj Ni estis malbenitaj. Mi estis amota. Ĝi estis aranĝota. Li estis baptota. Ili estis batotaj. Ni kunvenis por diskuti niajn aferojn. Mi foriras, sed mi baldaŭ revenos. Mi donis al li libron, sed li ĝin redonis al mi hodiaŭ. Tiu ĉi glaso estas rompebla, sed tiu estas nerompebla. Ŝi estas virino kredinda kaj honorinda. La lernanto estas nekredinda. Mia plumo estas fleksebla, sed via plumo ne estas fleksebla. Montru al mi la leteron ; eble mi povos helpi al vi. Li donis monereton al la almozulo. La kuiristo dormis pace en la kuirejo. La tubeto ne kiun li metas la cigaron por ĝiu fumi estas cigaringo. La knabo estas en la lernejo kaj lia fratino estas en la preĝejo. Mi portas mian monujon en la poŝo de mia surtuto. La Angloj loĝas en Anglujo (or Anglolando) kaj la Italoj en Italujo. La plumo estas en la plumingo, kaj la fingringo kuŝas sur la tablo. La alumetujo enhavas alumetojn, kaj la bombonujo enhavas bombonojn.

LESSON 22.—COMPOSITION.

If I had (should have) received the book, I would return it. If he loved you (now) he would tell you the truth. When she was (had been) very diligent the mother praised her. It is necessary that you should have finished (may have finished) my book before I return (shall return). When the priest will come, tell him the truth. They do not wish to give us the newspaper. Tell him that he should answer me. I think that I shall come to-morrow. A true friend is (becomes) known in danger. By a kind act one can always attain much more than by rude force. I shall go away to-day, because John awaits me. The lady spoke affably to us. He stood before the door of the church with a friend. The fallacy of your speech was quite evident. What (that which) will displease my father will displease me, sir. The (royal) prince related the whole matter to his father. A bird caught is better than a lion about to be caught. If I were (should be) good, I should be happy. A month ago my aunt visited me. The wife of the laundryman saw the wife of the doctor and the wife of the bootmaker yesterday in the theatre. He tore (in pieces) the book and then he threw it about in the street, because he was very angry. He is very credulous, but his wife is an idle and chattering (woman). A pound, shilling, penny, florin, dollar and franc are coins (pieces of money).

VOCABULARY FOR LESSONS 23 & 24.

Admiri,	To admire.	*Ŝipo,*	Ship.
Akiri,	To acquire.	*Estr*	(see prefixes, etc.).
Amuzi,	To amuse.		
Analizi,	To analyse.	*Placo,*	{ A public place.
Anonci,	To announce.		
Ataki,	To attack.	*Estimi,*	To esteem.
Razi,	To shave.	*Saĝa,*	Wise.
Ludi,	To play.	*Il*	(see prefixes, etc.).
Ĉasi,	To chase.		
Rimarki,	To remark.	*Falĉi*	To mow.
Ricevi,	To receive.	*Ŝafo,*	Sheep.
Ec	(see prefixes, etc.).	*Matura,*	{ Ripe (full-grown).
Telegramo,	Telegram.	*Ul*	(see prefixes, etc.).
Ŝlosi,	To lock.		
Tranĉi,	To cut.	*Mensogo,*	{ Falsehood. Lie.
Morti,	To die.		
Enterigi,	{ To inter. To bury.	*Germanoj,*	Germans.
		Danoj,	Danes.
Dimanĉo,	Sunday.	*Rusoj,*	Russians.
Rezervi,	To reserve.	*Katoliko,*	Catholic.
Lito,	Bed.	*Luterano,*	Lutheran.
Alveni,	To arrive.	*Kalvinano,*	Calvinist.
Koro,	Heart.	*Kristano,*	Christian.
Gratuli,	{ To felicitate. To congratu- late.	*Vidvo,*	Widower.
		Nepo,	Grandson.
		Ho,	Oh !

Kiel eble plej frue, as early (as soon) as possible.
Kiel eble plej rapide, as quickly as possible.
Tago de naskiĝo, birthday (anniversary).

LESSON 23.—TRANSLATION.

Mi estas amanta. Li estas skribanta. Ŝi estas kantanta. Mi estas admirinta. Ni estas akirintaj.

Ili estas amuzintaj. Li estas analizinta. Mi estas amuzonta. Ŝi estas anonconta. Ili estas atakontaj. Mi estis atendanta. Li estis razanta. Ŝi estis ludanta. Ili estis ĉasantaj. Mi estis aminta. Ni estis fumintaj. Li estis dancinta. Li estis ŝtelinta. Mi estis amonta. Ili estis rimarkontaj. Ni estis ricevontaj. La hundo kaj la kato vivas en granda amikeco. Mi deziras lin vidi, kiel eble plej frue. (Telegramoj): (1). Venu (al mi kiel eble) plej rapide, Johano mortis, enterigo dimanĉe. (2). Rezervu ĉambron kun du litoj, mi alvenos lundon nokte naŭ (horo). (3). (Mi sendas al vi mian) plej koran gratulon por Via naskiĝa tago. La heroeco de la ŝipestro tre plaĉis al la reĝo kaj la reĝido. La pastro amas tiun ĉi knabon por lia boneco kaj honesteco sed li malestimas lian fraton pro lia malsaĝeco. Ŝafido estas nematura ŝafo, kaj katido estas nematura kato. Vi estas mensogulo kaj li estas timulo. Germanoj, Danoj kaj Rusoj kiuj loĝas en Anglujo (Anglolando) estas Anglujanoj, sed ili ne estas Angloj. Katolikoj, Luteranoj kaj Kalvinanoj estas kristanoj. La maljuna vidvino amas siajn nepinojn. Ŝlosu la pordon, kaj donu al mi la ŝlosilon. Per razilo ni razas, per tranĉilo ni tranĉas kaj per falĉilo ni falĉas.

LESSON 24.—COMPOSITION.

I am loved (am being loved). You (sing.) are (now) named. It is (now) found. They are (now being) stolen. I have been loved. He has been seen. We have been paid. She has been drowned. She is (about) to be loved. They are (about) to be named. You (pl.) are (about) to be deceived. He was (about) to be punished.* I was named.* He was clothed (dressed).* We were seen.* They were pillaged (robbed).* He had been loved.* You (pl.) had

* All these refer to a particular time, when something else took place.

been photographed. They had been blessed. We had been cursed. I was (about) to be loved. It was (about) to be arranged. He was (about) to be baptised. They were (about) to be beaten. We assembled in order to discuss our affairs. I am going away, but I.will return soon. I gave him a book, but he returned it to me to-day. This glass is breakable, but that is unbreakable. She is a woman worthy of belief and honour. The pupil is not worthy of belief. My pen is flexible, but your pen is not (flexible). Show me the letter, possibly, I shall be able to help you. He gave a small coin to the beggar. The chef slept peacefully in the kitchen. The little tube into which he puts the cigar in order to smoke it is a cigar-holder. The boy is in the schoolroom, and his sister is in the church. I carry my purse in my overcoat pocket. The English inhabit (reside in) England and the Italians in Italy. The pen is in the penholder, and the thimble is on (lies on) the table. The match box contains matches, and the bonbon-box contains bonbons.

VOCABULARY FOR LESSONS 25 & 26.

Plori,	To weep.	*Ist*	(see prefixes, etc.).
Ŝpari,	{ To be careful. To spare.	*Drogo,*	Drug.
Suferi,	To suffer.	*Aĵ*	(see prefixes. etc.).
Sukcesi,	To succeed.		
Peni,	To try.	*Deŝiri,*	To tear off.
Venĝi,	To avenge.	*Pantalono,*	{ Pantaloon. Trousers.
Savi,	To save.		
Peli,	To expel.	*Spite,*	In spite of.
Marŝi,	To march.	*Tia, kia,*	{ Such as (it is).
Ĥemio,	Chemistry.		

Ul	(see prefixes, etc.).	*Nepo,*	Grandson.
Uzi,	To use.	*Estr*	(see prefixes, etc.).
Okazo,	Occurrence. Occasion.	*Regimento,* *Soldato,*	Regiment. Soldier.
Violono,	Violin.	*Okupi,*	To occupy.
Violonĉelo,	Violoncello.	*Urbo,*	City, town.
Pra,	Great-Grand (relationship).	*Pacienco,*	Patience.

Paŝo post paŝo, — Step by step.
Tago post tago, — Day by day (day after day).
Per malmultaj vortoj, — In a few words.
Post malmultaj tagoj, — In a few days.

LESSON 25.—TRANSLATION.

Mi estos amanta. Li estos skribanta. Ni estos legantaj. Ŝi estos ploranta. Li estos aminta. Vi (pl.) estos ŝparintaj. Ili estos malŝparintaj. Mi estos suferinta. Ili estos sukcesontaj. Ni estos penontaj. Li estos trinkonta la vinon. Mi estos amata. Li estos nomata. Ŝi estos trompata. Ĝi estos trovata. Ŝi estos amita. Vi (sing.) estos venĝita. Li estos benita. Li estos malbenita. Mi estos amota. Ili estos savotaj. Vi (pl.) estos forpelotaj. Li marŝis paŝo post paŝo. Okulo, okulisto. Ĥemio, ĥemiisto. Drogo, drogisto. Mia frato havis deŝirajojn en sia pantalono. Li foriris spite mi. Mi donis al li la libron tian, kia ĝi estis. Mia onklo estas riĉulo, sed mi estas malriĉulo. Mi vidis belulon kaj belulinon en la teatro. Mi penos fari uzon el la okazo. Mi rakontos al vi la historion per malmultaj vortoj. La violonisto amas sian violonon, sed la violonĉelisto ne ŝatas sian violonĉelon. La infano disverŝis la inkon sur mian naztukon. Skribisto ne verkas librojn, li transskribas paperojn (dokumentojn); sed verkisto verkas librojn, libretojn, k.t.p. La provincestroj de tiuj ĉi provincoj estas maljustaj. La filoj, filinoj, nepoj, nepinoj, pranepoj kaj pranepinoj de reĝo estas reĝidoj. La regimentestro kaj la soldatoj de la regimento okupos la urbon. Estu bona, kaj havu paciencon. Pardonu al mi, mi petas, sinjoro.

LESSON 26.—COMPOSITION.

I am loving. He is writing. She is singing. I have admired (literally, I am having admired). We have acquired. They have amused. He has analyzed. I am about to amuse. She is about to announce. They are about to attack. I was waiting. He was shaving. She was playing. They were hunting. I had loved. We had smoked. He had danced. He had stolen. I was about to love. They were about to remark. We were about to receive. The dog and the cat live in great friendship. I desire to see him as early as possible. (Telegrams) :—(1). Come to me as quickly as possible, John is dead (has died) ; interment (on) Sunday. (2). Reserve room with two beds, I will arrive Monday night (àt) 9 o'clock. (3). I send you my most hearty congratulation for (on) your birthday. The heroism of the (ship) captain (very) pleased the King and the prince (the King's son). The pastor loves this boy on account of his goodness and honesty, but he despises his brother on account of his foolishness. A lamb is an immature sheep and a kitten is an immature cat. You are a liar and he is a coward. Germans, Danes and Russians who reside (dwell) in England are English inhabitants, but they are not English (men) Catholics, Lutherans and Calvinists are Christians. The old widow loves her granddaughters. Lock the door, and give me the key. We shave with a razor, we cut with a knife, and we mow with a scythe.

VOCABULARY FOR LESSONS 27 & 28.

Pasi,	To pass.	*Flugi,*	To fly.
Ig	(see prefixes, etc.).	*Naĝi,*	To swim.
		Rampi,	To creep.
Kelnero,	Waiter.	*Fremdulo,*	Foreigner.
Pipro,	Pepper.	*Konfesi,*	To confess.
Salo,	Salt.	*Kulpo,*	Fault.
Forko,	Fork.	*Parkere,*	By heart.
Sano,	Health.	*Perdi,*	To lose.
Vanta,	{Frivolous. Vain.	*Ŝati,*	To like.
		Demeti,	To put off.
Apud,	Near.	*Surmeti,*	To put on.
Sata,	Satiated.	*Ventroparo-*	Ventrilo-
Sen,	{Without. Less.	*listo,*	quist.
		Trančileto,	Penknife.
Senutila,	Useless.	*Sekvi,*	To follow.
Leciono,	Lesson.	*Volumo,*	Volume.
Kuri,	To run.	*Ŝajni,*	To seem.

Ju pli—des pli, The more—the more.

Tiom, kiom, As many (much) as.

For (Prefix to verbs), Far, away, as *Forkuri,* To run away.

El (Prefix to verbs), From, out of, as *Eliri,* To go out of, to go away from.

This Prefix also denotes that something has been done very well, thoroughly, completely, as *Li elesploris la landon,* he explored the land thoroughly.

LESSON 27.—TRANSLATION.

Pasigu al mi la akvon, mi petas. Kelnero, pasigu al mi la pipron kaj la salon. Kiam mi estis tie, mi vidis knabinon ĉe la pordego. Alportu al ni tri forkojn. Mi vidas multe da homoj en la strato. Li parolis al mi pri mia sano, kaj mi estas tre danka al li. Ju pli mi ĝin legas, des pli mi ĝin ŝatas. Tiuj ĉi

libroj estas vantaj kaj senutilaj. Li lernas sian
lecionon, sed ŝi ĝin ellernas. Tiu ĉi skatoleto enhavas
miajn leterojn. La lernejestro kaj la lernanto estas
en la lernejo. Hundoj forkuras, birdoj forflugas,
fiŝoj fornaĝas kaj rampaĵoj forrampas.* Mi estas
fremdulo en fremda lando. Ŝi aĉetas tiom da libroj
kiom mi. La knabo konfesis la kulpon kaj ploris tre
laŭte. Li lernu parkere la lecionon. Lia ludo estis
tre bona, sed li perdis sian tutan monon. Respondu
al mi kaj diru al mi la tutan veron. Demetu vian
ĉapelon kaj sidiĝu. Surmetu vian surtuton kaj foriru
de tie ĉi. Mi vidis ventroparoliston hieraŭ en la
teatro. Mi trovis tranĉileton sub la tablo. Pasigu al
li la libron, kiu estas apud vi. Li prenu tion, kion li
bezonas. Jen estas la libro, mi sendos al vi la
sekvantan volumon morgaŭ. Ili manĝadis ĝis sato.
Vi ŝajnas ĉiam bela al mi, patrino mia! La infano
manĝis la restaĵon de la kuko, kaj tial li ridis.

LESSON 28.—COMPOSITION.

I shall be loving. He will be writing. We shall
be reading. She will be weeping. He will have loved.
You (pl.) will have economised. They will have squan-
dered. I shall have suffered. They will be about to
succeed. We shall be about to try. He will be
about to drink the wine. I shall be loved. He will
be named. She will be deceived. It will be found.
She will have been loved. You (sing.) will have been
avenged. He will have been blessed. He will have
been cursed. I shall be about to be loved. They
will be about to be saved. You (pl.) will be about to
be driven away. He marched step by step. Eye,
oculist. Chemistry, chemist. Drug, druggist. My

---

* These verbs denote the different means by which animals,
etc., escape from foes.

brother had rents (torn places) in his trousers. He went away in spite of me. I gave him the book, such as it was. My uncle is a rich man, but I am a poor man. I saw a handsome man and a beautiful woman in the theatre. I will try to make use of the occasion. I shall relate to you the history in a few words. The violinist loves his violin, but the violoncellist does not like his violoncello. The child spilled the ink on my handkerchief. A writer does not write books, he transcribes papers (documents), but an author (Verkisto) works (writes) books, pamphlets, etc. The rulers (governors) of these provinces are unjust. The sons, daughters, grandsons, granddaughters, great grandsons and great granddaughters of a King are of Royal blood (descendants of the King). The chief (head) of the regiment and the soldiers of the regiment will occupy the city. Be good and have patience. Pardon me, if you please, sir.

LESSON 29.—COMPOSITION.

Pass me the water, if you please. Waiter, pass me the pepper and the salt. When I was there, I saw a little girl at the gate. Bring us three forks. I see many people in the street. He spoke to me about my health and I am very thankful to him. The more I read it, the more I like it. These books are frivolous and useless. He learns his lesson, but she studies it thoroughly. This little box contains my letters. The teacher and the scholar are in the schoolroom. Dogs run away, birds fly away, fish swim away, and reptiles crawl away. I am a stranger in a strange land. She buys as many books as I. The boy confessed the fault and wept very loudly. Let him learn, by heart, the lesson. His play was very good, but he lost all his money. Answer me and tell me the whole truth.

Take off your hat and be seated. Put on your overcoat and go away from here. I saw a ventriloquist yesterday in the theatre. I found a pen-knife under the table. Pass him the book which is near you. Let him take what (that which) he needs (requires). Here is the book ; 1 will send the following volume to you to-morrow. They continued eating to (until) satiety. You seem (appear) always beautiful to me, mother (dear). The child ate the remainder of the cake, (and) that is why (therefore) he laughed.

EXERCISES ON THE CORRELATIVE WORDS (Pages 42 & 43).

1. *Ia amiko vin helpos.*

   1. Some friend will help you.

   Mi havis ian ideon kiel ĝin fari.

   I had some idea how to do it.

2. *Ial li subite forlasis Londonon.*

   2. For some reason he suddenly left London.

3. *Kiam ajn vi povos min viziti, estos konvene al mi.*

   3. Anytime that you are able to visit me will be convenient to me.

   Venu hodiaŭ, ar iam morgaŭ estos tro malfrue.

   Come to-day, for anytime to-morrow will be too late.

4. *Mi ne povis trovi mian libron ie en la ĉambro.*

   4. I could not find my book anywhere in the room.

   Ĉu vi metis ĝin ien ?

   Did you put it anywhere ?

5. *Iel li sukcesas en ĉio.*

   5. Somehow he succeeds in everything.

F

6. *Ies perdo ne estas ĉiam ies gajno.*

6. Anyone's loss is not always somebody's gain.

7. *Io estis sub la tablo, sed mi ne povis vidi ion tie.*

7. Something was under the table, but I could not see anything there.

Morgaŭ mi sendos al vi ion belan.

To-morrow I will send you something beautiful.

Li vidis ion kion li tre amis.

He saw something which he liked very much.

8. *Mi iom komprenas tion, kion vi volas diri.*

8. I understand a little of what you wish to say.

La vetero estas iom pli varma.

The weather is somewhat warmer.

9. *Ĉu iu estos tie?*

9. Will there be anyone there?

Mi ne vidos iun tie.

I shall not see any one there.

10. *Ĉiu aĝo havas siajn devojn.*

10. Each age has its duties.

Mi konis ĉiun viron, kiun mi renkontis.

I knew every man whom I met.

11. *Kial vi silentis?*

11. Why were you silent?

Ĉial tio estas la plej bona.

For every reason that is the best.

12. *Mi ĉiam respondas al viaj leteroj.*

12. I always reply to your letters.

Ĉiam skribu legeble.

Always write legibly.

Ĉiam sendu al mi, se vi estos malsana.

Always send to me if you should be ill.

Ĉiam pripensu antaŭ ol vi parolas.

Always consider before you speak.

13. *Ĉie mi trovis amikojn.*

13. Everywhere I found friends.

Akvo, akvo ĉie, sed eĉ ne unu akvero por trinki.

Water, water every-where, but not a drop to drink.

14. *Ni helpos la lernan-tojn ĉiel.*

14. We will help the pupils in every way.

15. *Ĉies ideo estis diversa.*

15. Each one's idea was different.

16. *Ĉio havas lokon propran, tial metu ĉion en ĝian pro-pran lokon.*

16. Everything has a proper place, there-fore put every-thing into its proper place.

17. *Ĉio kion mi havas estas ankaŭ (la) via.*

17. All I have is also yours.

18. *Preskaŭ ĉiu amas sin mem.*

18. Nearly everyone loves himself.

Mi legis ĉion zorge, antaŭ ol mi ĝin sendis al li.

I read each one care-fully before I sent it to him.

El ĉiuj miaj amikoj, li estas la plej bona.

Of all my friends, he is the best.

Ŝi legis ĉiun libron, kiun ŝi povis ricevi.

She read every book which she could get.

19. *Kia lingvo ĝi estas!*

19. What a language it is!

Kian leteron vi skribis?

What kind of letter did you write?

Kiaj ĉarmaj infanoj estas (la) viaj!

What charming chil-dren yours are!

Kiajn belajn librojn mi legis.

What beautiful books I read (past).

20. *Kial vi ne skribis al li?*

20. Why did you not write to him?

Kial vi ne venos al nia kunveno?

Why will you not come to our meeting?

21. *Kiam ni iros Lon-donon?*

21. When shall we go to London?

	Kiam ni estos finintaj nian laboron.	When we have finished our work.
22.	*Kie estas la poŝt-oficejo?*	22. Where is the post office?
23.	*Kiel vi elparolas "aŭ"?*	23. How do you pronounce "aŭ"?
	Kiel "ow" en la angla vorto "cow."	Like "ow" in "cow."
24.	*Kies libro estas tiu ĉi?*	24. Whose book is this?
	Kies plumon vi uzas?	Whose pen are you using?
	Mi vidis kampon en kies mezo staris du arboj.	I saw a field in the middle of which stood two trees.
25.	*Kio iras rapide? La tempo.*	25. What goes quickly? Time.
	Kion li volis montri al vi?	What did he wish to show you?
26.	*Kiom da ĉevaloj estis tie?*	26. How many horses were there?
	Kiom kostas tio?	How much does that cost?
	Je kioma horo vi venos al mi?	At what o'clock will you come to my house?
27.	*Kiu parolas Esper-anton?*	27. Who speaks Esper-anto?
	Kiu estos tie?	Who will be there?
	Kiuj estas la tagoj de la semajno?	Which are the days of the week?
	Kion vi bezonas?	What do you want (need)?
	La librojn, kiujn vi pruntos al mi.	The books that you will lend me.
28.	*Nenia antaŭa sperto estas necesa.*	28. No previous experience is necessary.

*Mi estis havinta nenian
antaŭan sperton.*

I had not had any
previous experience.

29. *Li nenial ĉesis skribi
al mi.*

29. For no $\begin{Bmatrix} \text{cause} \\ \text{reason} \end{Bmatrix}$ he
ceased writing to me.

30. *Neniam? Estas longa
tempo.*
*Mi neniam skribas
longajn leteroin.*
*Mi neniam âcetas
malkarajn librojn.*

30. Never? It is a long
time.
I never write long
letters.
I never buy cheap
books.

31. *Nenie, oni min
komprenis.*
*Nenie oni povis trovi
mian hundon.*

31. Nowhere did they
understand me.
Nowhere could they
find my dog.

32. *Ŝi neniel povis kom-
preni tion, kion li
skribis en alia lingvo.*

32. She could nohow
understand what he
wrote in another
language.

*Sen Esperanto li
neniel povis kom-
prenigi sin.*

Without Esperanto he
could nohow make
himself understood.

33. *I e s devo estas
nenies (devo).*

33. Anybody's duty is
nobody's (duty).

34. *Nenio estas preta.*
*Ĉu vi havas nenion
por diri al mi?*

34. Nothing is ready.
Have you nothing to
say to me?

35. *Li havas neniom.*

35. He has nothing at
all.

36. *Neniu estis apud la
pordo.*
Neniu parolas al mi.
*Ĉu vi neniun vidis
tie kiun vi konis?*

36. No one was near the
door.
No one speaks to me.
Did you see no one
there whom you
knew?

Mi neniun vidis ĉe vi.

I saw no one at your
house.

37. *Tia ripetado enuas min.*
En tiaj okazoj ĉiam mankas io.

37. Such repetition annoys me.
On these occasions something is always {wanting} {missing.}

Mi neniam vidis tian aferon.

I never saw such an affair.

38. *Ĉar li ne respondas al vi, ne kredu, ke li ne volas respondi; tial mi al vi konsilas skribi al li.*

38. Because he does not reply to you, do not believe that he does not wish to reply ; therefore I advise you to write to him.

39. *Tiam ni povos iri al la kunveno.*

39. Then we shall be able to go to the meeting.

Mi vizitos vin tiam, kiam vi estos preta.

I will visit you (then) when you are (will be) ready.

40. *Tie vi trovos multe da amikoj.*
Mi iros tien, kiam mi ricevos vian leteron.
Miaj amikoj loĝas tie ĉi.
Ĉu viaj fratoj venos tien ĉi?

40. There you will find many friends.
I shall go there when I (shall) receive your letter.
My friends live here.
Will your brothers come here ?

41. *Se estus tiel, vi devus skribi al li.*

41. If it is so (should be), you should write to him.

Mi sentas min tiel malfeliĉa, ke vi devus reveni.
Kiam vi skribis tiel ?

I feel so unhappy that you should come back.
When did you write like that ?

42. *Mi neniam prenas ties konsilon.*

42. I never take such a one's advice.

43. *Ĉu vi parolas pri tio ?*

Mi neniam aŭdis tion.

Tio ĉi estas malkredinda.

Vi devus memori tion ĉi.

43. Are you speaking about that ?

I never heard that.

This is unworthy of belief.

You should remember this.

44. *Tiom estas malfacile memori.*

44. So much is difficult to remember.

45. *Mi loĝis en tiu urbo.*

Ĉu mi montris al vi tiun leteron ?

Kie kreskas tiuj floroj ?

Ĉu vi ricevis tiujn librojn ?

Tiu ĉi ringo estas por vi.

Mi neniam forgesos tiun ĉi regulon.

Tiuj ĉi hundoj estas tre grandaj.

Mi aĉetos tiujn ĉi librojn.

45. I lived in that town.

Did I show you that letter ?

Where do those flowers grow ?

Did you receive those books ?

This ring is for you.

I shall never forget this rule.

These dogs are very large.

I shall buy these books.

PART III.—CONVERSATIONS.

Bonan tagon, sinjoro. — Good day, sir.

Kiel vi fartas? — How are you? How do you do?

Tre bone, sinjoro, mi dankas vin. — Very well, sir, thank you.

Mi ĝojas ke mi vin vidas en bona sano. — I rejoice to see you in good health.

Vi estas tre ĝentila. — You are very kind (polite).

Al ni estas varme. — We are warm.

Al ili estas malvarme. — They are cold.

Mi malsatas. — I am hungry.

Li tre soifas. — He is very thirsty.

Kia estas la vetero? — How (what kind) is the weather?

Ni havos belegan tagon. — We shall have a beautiful day.

Tiom pli bone. — So much the better.

Kiu frapas? Kiu estas tie? — Who knocks? Who is there?

Estas mi. Malfermu. — It is I. Open.

Envenu. La ŝlosilo estas en la seruro. — Come in. The key is in the lock.

Vi estas prava. Li estas malprava. — You are right. He is wrong.

Pli bone estas agi malfrue ol neniam. — Better (to act) late than never.

Sidiĝu, mi petas. — Take a seat, please.

Mi vin petas sidiĝi. — I pray you to be seated (take a seat).

Mi tie estos tiel baldaŭ, kiel vi.	I will be there as soon as you.
Vi vin trompas, ne povas esti.	You deceive yourself, it cannot be.
Mi vin certigas, ke jes.	I assure you that it is so.
Vizaĝo kontraŭ vizaĝo.	Face to face.
Brako ĉe brako.	Arm in arm.
Koro ĉe koro.	Heart to heart.
Mano en mano.	Hand in hand.
Donu al mi vian manon.	Give me your hand.
Kion vi diras pri tio?	What do you say about that?
Vi povas kredi al mi.	You may (can) believe me.
Mi estas certa je tio.	I am certain of that.
Ne, ne estas eble.	No, it is not possible.
Ĉu vi konsentas al tio?	Do you agree to that?
Jes, certe kun plezuro.	Yes, certainly, with pleasure.
Vi alvenas ĝustatempe.	You arrive just in time.
Vi jam diris tion ĉi trifoje.	You (have) said this three times already.
Li venis nur unufoie.	He came only once.
Ekbruligu la fajron, la kandelon.	Light the fire, the candle.
La fajro brulas malbone.	The fire burns badly.
Mi bezonas inkujon.	I require an inkstand.
Ĉu vi min komprenas?	Do you understand me?
Jes, sinjoro, mi vin komprenas.	Yes, sir, I understand you.
Kial vi ne respondis?	Why did you not answer?
Mi ne aŭdis tre bone.	I did not hear very well.
Ni laboru kaj esperu.	Let us labour and hope.
Mi atendas viajn ordonojn.	I await your orders.
Via ideo estas tre bona.	Your idea is very good.
Mi kredas, ke vi faros bone.	I believe that you will do well.
Kion vi bezonas?	What do you want (need)?

Mi bezonas kandelingon.	I want a candlestick.
Nenion mi bezonas.	I want nothing.
Jen estas teo, prenu iom da ĝi.	Here is tea, take some of it.
Mi havas cigarojn, ĉu vi deziras iom?	I have cigars, do you want some?
Ĉu vi havas monon? Mi havas.	Have you money? I have.
Ĉu vi volas lakton aŭ kremon?	Do you wish (for) milk or cream?
Mi preferas kremon.	I prefer cream.
Kiom kostas tiu ĉi objekto?	How much does this object cost?
Ĝi kostas dek ŝilingojn.	It costs ten shillings.
Kien vi iras tiel rapide?	Where are you going so quickly?
Nenien (mi iras).	(I am going) Nowhere.
Kian aĝon li havas?	How old is he?
Li havas dek ok jarojn.	He is eighteen years.
Li estas maljunulo de sesdek jaroj.	He is an old man of sixty years.
Antaŭ unu semajno, antaŭ unu monato.	A week ago, a month ago.
Post du horoj, post ok tagoj.	In two hours, in a week.
Kion vi farus, se vi estus mi?	What would you do if you were I?
Mi ne scias kiel vin danki por la granda servo.	I do not know how to thank you for the great service.
Kia estas via opinio?	What is your opinion?
Mi ne scias bone.	I don't well know.
Kiam ni haltos por matenmanĝi?	When shall we stop to (have) breakfast?
Post unu horo ni estos en la stacidomo.	In (after) one hour we shall be at the station.
Rigardu la maljunan sinjoron, kiu legas.	Look at the old man who is reading.

Tiu, kiu havas la harojn nigrajn ?	He who has black hair ?
Jes, kian aĝon li havas?	Yes, what age is he ?
Li havas ne malpli ol okdek jarojn.	He is not less than 80 years.
Ili estas nur tri aŭ kvar.	They are only three or four.
Ŝi estas tre kolera.	She is very angry.
Jen li kantas, jen li ploras.	Sometimes he sings, sometimes he weeps.
Sendu lin al mi kiam ajn li venos.	Send him to me whenever he comes.
Kiu estas en la domo ?	Who is in the house ?
Kian tempon de jaro vi preferas ?	What time of the year do you prefer ?
Kia ĉarma infano !	What a charming child .
Kia bela domo !	What a beautiful house !
Li ne povas trovi la vortaron.	He cannot find the dictionary.
Ĉu li fumas ?	Does he smoke ?
Mi lin konas fame.	I know him by reputation.
Fermu la pordon.	Close the door.
Ŝlosu la pordon.	Lock the door.
Kiam li alvenos ?	When will he come ?
Mi havas ion por diri al vi.	I have something to say to you.
Ni havas multe por fari	We have much to do.
Mi venos la lundon plej proksiman.	I shall come next Monday.
Li mortis la lastan Ĵaŭdon.	He died last Thursday.
Estas du infanoj en la ĉambro apuda.	There are two children in the next room.
Pasigu al mi la panon, mi petas.	Pass me the bread, if you please.
Pasigu al mi la mustardon.	Pass me the mustard.
Pasigu al mi la salaton.	Pass me the salad.
Kelnero, donu al mi la akvon.	Waiter ! give me (the) water.

EN RESTORACIO.

Kelnero, ni volas tagmanĝi, sed se estus eble, en loko senbrua, ĉar mi ne amas manĝi surdigata per la rulado de la veturiloj kaj per ĉiuj bruoj de la strato. Tie ĉi ni estas kvazaŭ ekstere.

La sinjoroj povus sin meti en kabineton apartan, sur la unuan etaĝon, ĉe la flanko de la korto ; ili nenian bruon aŭdus tie.

Nu, jes ; ni estos almenaŭ pli trankvilaj ol tie ĉi. Montru al ni la vojon, kaj servu al ni rapide, ĉar mi mortas de malsato. Vi ŝanĝos la tablotukon, tiu ĉi ne estas tre pura.

Ho mi ĝin tuj ŝanĝos. Kiom da manĝilaroj ?

Tri, ĉar ni atendas iun, li eĉ devus jam esti alveninta. Nu, ni legu la karton de la manĝaĵoj. *Supoj senviandaj :* vermiĉelo en lakto, okzala supo, supo Parmentier (terpoma), tapioko en lakto, supo fazeola. — *Viandaj supoj :* buljono kun makaronoj, tapioko en buljono, ĵulieno (buljono kun diversaj legomoj), konsomeo, supo testuda.

Mi ne manĝos supon. Diru al mi kion oni skribis pri fiŝoj.

Ni povas havi : salmon, truton, haringon, karpon kaj ezokon.

Mi volonte manĝus angilon ; sed ĉar la karto ĝin ne proponas, ĉu ni ne povus komenci per ostroj ? Se vi volas supon, vi ĝin manĝos poste.

Jes, mi aprobas, ni prenu ostrojn kun bona botelo da vino el Chablis (Ŝabli).

Decidite mi ne manĝos supon. Ni elektu ian viandon. Jen : bovaĵo rostita aŭ rosbifo, bovaĵo bolita, bovidaĵo kun okzalo, renoj de ŝafido, bifstekoj, kotletoj de ŝafido, de ŝafideto, de bovido, de porko ; femuro de ŝafido (rostita aŭ bolita), kapo de bovido kun saŭco vinagra, ŝinko el Jorko, viandoj malvarmaj.

Kaj pri kortobirdoj ?

Meleagrino rostita, ansero kun kaŝtanoj, kokino kun rizo, anaso kun olivoj, kokido rostita.

Nu, mi prenos renojn de ŝafido post la ostroj.

Mi ankaŭ. Kelnero, ĉu viaj porcioj estas dikaj ?

Ho, jes, sinjoro, unu tre sufiĉas por du personoj.

Se ni prenus ian legomon post la renoj; kion vi diros pri tio ĉi ?

Volonte ; ni vidu la legomojn. Estas sur la karto : pureo de terpomoj ; flora brasiko kun oleo ; pizetoj france kuiritaj ; asparagoj kun blanka saŭco ; spinaco kun viandsuko, terpomoj frititaj.

Mi rimarkigas al vi, kara amiko, ke ĝis nun ni ĝuste elektis nur du manĝaĵojn : la ostrojn kaj la renojn de ŝafido. Ŝajnas al mi ke vi alkondukas nin iom tro rapide al la legomoj. Ĉu ni ne povus preni ovojn post la ostroj, ĉar ni ne manĝos supon ?

Jes, vi estas prava ; sed ni komencu atakante la manĝaĵetojn kiuj estas sur la tablo ; pasigu al mi la rafanojn, mi petas. Mi ne povas pli atendi. Vi ne prenas iom da ili !

Ne, dankon ; mi preferas la olivojn. Nun, se ni decidus la demandon pri la ovoj, kiel vi amas ilin ?

Ho ! en ĉiuj manieroj : en la ŝelo, malmolajn, kunmiksitajn, platigitajn, poŝumitajn, frititajn.

Sed ĉu vi amas ovaĵon ?

Ho, jes, multe.

Ĉu ni petus pri unu ?

Tre volonte ; ni prenu ovaĵon kun herbetoj post la ostroj.

Ni do havas la ostrojn, la ovaĵon kun herbetoj kaj la renojn.

Jes, nun ni bezonas legomon. Mi proponas verdajn fazeolojn.

Tre bone, mi amas ilin multe. Sed iom da ĉasaĵo ne malplaĉus al mi poste.

Kian strangan menuon ni kombinas tiel ! Kio estas notita sur la karto pri ĉasaĵo ?

Leporo rostita, perdriko kaj fazano.

Mi elektas perdrikon, ĉar mi manĝis leporon hieraŭ kaj mi havas abomenon por la fazano.

Nu, mi imitos vian ekzemplon. Sed sâjnas al mi ke, poste, iom da salato estos necesega.

Nu, elektu ni unu.

Kelnero, kiajn salatojn vi havas ?

Latukon pomforman, latukon romanan, endivon, leontodon, duceton.

PRI LA TEMPERATURO, LA SEZONOJ KAJ LA MONATOJ.

Inter la dekdu monatoj, el kiuj konsistas jaro, kiun vi preferas ?

Unue vi devus demandi min, ĉu mi pliamas la varmon aŭ la malvarmon ; ĉar, kompreneble, mi devos elekti monaton printempan, someran, aŭtunan aŭ vintran, konforme je mia prefero.

Diru do al mi kian temperaturon vi plivolas. La sekan aŭ la malsekan ? la varman aŭ la malvarman ? la varmegan aŭ la glacian ?

Vi mokas min, kara mia. Sed mi senŝerce diros al vi, ke el ĉiuj sezonoj de jaro mi preferas la printempon kaj la majan monaton. Marto estas ofte iom malvarma, ŝanĝema, venta, pluva. Aprilo apenaŭ komencas montri al ni la unuajn ridetojn de la suno Sed en Majo vere reviviĝas la naturo : la arboj malfermas siajn burĝonojn, kovras sin per folioj kaj floroj ; unuvorte ĉiuj kreskaĵoj kaj vegetaĵoj ĉarmas la rigardon, parfumas la aeron kaj ĉirkaŭ si disdonas impreson de vekiĝo kaj ĝojo.

Ho kiel poeta vi estas ! Sed kelkfoje la maja monato estas tre diferenca de la bela pentro, kiun vi faris pri ĝi. Oni ofte devas atendi ĝis Junio, por vidi la naturon sub la brilaj koloroj, kiujn al ĝi vi alskribis.

Jes, mi ĝin konfesas. Sed en Majo oni ricevas pli fortan sentaĵon de aliformiĝo kaj renaskiĝo en la naturo.

Kontraŭe mi preferas la dormadon de la naturo, ĝian ŝajnan mortintecon dum la vintro. Ĝi tiel respon- das pli bone al mia karaktero malĝoja kaj melankolia. Mi amas longe revadi, promenante tra la nudigita kamparo, kovrita per ĝia mantelo de brilega neĝo. Estas por mi plezuro rigardi sur la vitrojn de mia fenestro la mil figuraĵojn sur ili desegnatajn de la ĝivro. Kiam mi trairas la senbruajn arbarojn, ŝajnas al mi, ke ili fariĝis silentaj por ne malhelpi al mia revado. Se la pluvo falas, la vento blovas, fajfas kaj furiozas, mi restas hejme, kaj atendas pacience la ĉeson de la pluvo, la kvietiĝon de la vento, sidante apud la fajro kaj fumante bonan cigaron aŭ cigareon kaj eĉ kelkafoje honegan pipon.

Alivorte vi evitas la pluvon kaj la venton de la vintro, sed vi amas la neĝon kiu vin frostigas ĝis la ostoj, la hajleton kiu vin blindigas, la ĝivron kiu falas de la arboj kaj blankigas vin kiel faruno, fine la glacion kiu faras vin gliti je ĉiu paŝo. Mi ne kalkulis la plezuron konstante tremadi aŭ sin kovri tiamaniere, ke oni ne povas pli movi sin. Mi ankaŭ forgesis la ĝojon eniĝi en la koton ĝis la maleoloj, post forta pluvego.

Kaj vi, Ludoviko! Vi diras nenion. Kian tempon de jaro vi preferas ?

Ho mi! mi havas guston tute diferencan de la via : la printempo ne plaĉas al mi pro sia karaktero ŝanĝema. Dum tiu sezono, oni scias neniam, ĉu oni devas preni la pluvombrelon aŭ la bastonon. La monatojn Novembron, Decembron, Januaron kaj eĉ Februaron mi ne ŝatas, tial ke mi pli ol ĉion malamas la malvarmon. Ĝi malvigligas kaj paralizas la spiriton. De alia flanko, la somero ne plaĉas al mi pli multe. En Julio kaj Aŭgusto, la varmo faras vin senzorga kaj maldiligenta ; oni perdas ĉiun agemon.

Mi preferas la aŭtunon kaj la du monatojn Septem-bron, Oktobron. En ili la vetero estas pli konstanta, la temperaturo pli agrabla kaj mezgrada. Oni ne timas ĉiam vidi siajn projektojn malhelpatajn de ia pluvego aŭ fulmotondro, kiel en la printempo kaj en la somero.

Dum la aŭtuno, vi povas vojaĝi en trankvileco ; la marŝo estas plezuro kaj nenian malutilon prezentas la ripozado ĉe la naturo. Kontraŭe, vi riskas ricevi sun-frapon se, en la somero, vi restadas sub la radiado de la suno, aŭ pneŭmonion, en la vintro, se vi haltadas kelkan tempon ekstere.

Sed vi kantis la indon de tiuj sezonoj. Permesu do ke mi pledu por la printempo, montrante ĝiajn ecojn.

Se ni komparos la sezonojn kun la vivo de la homo, ni trovos ke la printempo respondas al la infaneco. Agrabla, ĉarma kiel tiu ĉi, la printempo havas ankaŭ ĝian kaprican kaj ŝanĝeman humoron : jen ridoj, jen ploroj senatendaj.

La somero respondas al la aĝo de la pasioj. La naturo tiam estas plena per elektro kaj fajro, kiel la vejnoj homaj en tiu periodo de la vivo : ĝi estas la tempo de la fulmotondroj kaj de la grandaj katastrofoj.

Pli certa, pli kvieta, pli mezura, la aŭtuno figuras la maturecon en la vivo. Ĝi ne estas la sezono de la floroj plej brilaj, sed ĝi estas la tempo de la fruktoj plej belaj kaj plej bongustaj. Persikoj, piroj, pomoj kaj vinberoj ĝojigas la vidadon kaj flatas la gustadon.

Se la verdeco de la arboj ne estas tiel freŝa kiel en la printempo, ĝi prezentas pli grandan riĉecon da nuancoj. La naturo ne uzas pli uniforme la verdon, ĝi prenas aliajn kolorilojn sur sian paletron kaj miksas la flavon, la ruĝon kaj eĉ la brunon kun la verdo de sia ĝistiama pentraĵo.

La aero pli seka ol en la printempo, pli pura kaj

malpeza ol en la somero, ne malvarma kiel en la vintro, estas multe pli saniga ol en la aliaj sezonoj.

Pro tiuj diversaj motivoj mi alskribas la superecon al la printempo.

POR SALUTI KAJ DEMANDI PRI LA SANO.

Mi deziras al vi bonan tagon, Sinjoro:

Bonan tagon, Sinjoro, kiel vi fartas?

Tre bone; mi dankas (vin).

Oni diris al mi ke vi estas malsana.

Ho ne, dankoj al Dio; mi neniam sanis pli bone ol de kelka tempo; se tio ĉi daŭriĝos, la kuracistoj ne gajnos multe de mi.

Benadu la ĉielon, ĉar la sano certe estas la plej grandvalora bono el ĉiuj. Se vi estus kiel mi en konstanta malsaneco, vi ankoraŭ pli multe ŝatus vian feliĉecon. Sed kiu venas tie, lamante kaj apoganto sin sur bastono? Ĉu ne estas nia amiko B?

Jes, estas li. La mizera rompis al si kruron antaŭ du monatoj kaj li marŝas ankoraŭ pene.

Bonveno al vi, amiko, mi ĵus sciiĝis la malfeliĉon, kiu okazis al vi. Kiel vi sanas nun?

Vi estas tre aminda. Nun mia stato estas pli ĝena ol dolora; sed, en la unuaj tagoj, mi suferis terure.

Ĉu via ĉarma familio estas en bona sano?

Mia edzino ĉiam havas sian feran sanon, sed unu el miaj infanoj kaŭzas al mi grandan maltrankvilecon; de kelkaj tagoj, ĝi havas mienon tre malbonan, ne havas pli apetiton kaj ĉiam plendas pri kapdoloroj.

Ha! kiu do el ili?

La plej juna. Ĝis nun ĝi estis tute sana kaj eĉ tre forta kompare kun sia aĝo.

Eble tio ĉi venas nur el tro granda kresko. La kreskado tre lacigas la infanojn kaj faras ilin pli malpli suferantaj, malsanetaj.

Tiuj ĉi estas precize la aferoj, kiujn al mi mem mi diras por trankviliĝi ; sed malgraŭ ĉio mi ne povas defendi min de kelka timo.

Estu pli saĝa kaj ne vidu danĝeron tie, kie nur estas afero natura, stato momenta kiun venkas ordinare ĉiuj infanoj sen ia el la komplikaĵoj, kiujn al si kreas via fantazio timigita.

Tion ĉi vi diras por trankviligi min kaj mi estas al vi tre danka pro ĝi, sed ĉar vi mem estas patro, vi certe komprenas ke viaj vortoj ne konvinkas min tute.

Nu, adiaŭ, amiko, faru mil salutojn al via frato, je mia nomo ; salutu vian patron de mi kaj prezentu mian respektan submetiĝon al via patrino.

Certe mi ĝin faros. De via flanko ne forgesu revoki min al la memoro de viaj gepatroj.

EN VOJAĜO KAJ EN SERĈADO DE LOĜEJO.

Rigardu do, Henriko, kian belan vidaĵon prezentas tiu kastelo, sidanta sur la supro de la monteto antaŭ ni. La senfrukteco de la pejzaĝo, la krutaĵoj, kiujn ĝi superas kaj la ŝtonegoj sur kiuj ĝi staras, donas al ĝi eksteron (or vidiĝon) de forteco kaj majesteco tute imponan.

Ĝi estas efektive tre impona sed ne malpli malĝojiga. Por nenio mi volus loĝadi en tiu nesto de aglo, tiom pli ke la kamparo ĉirkaŭanta ŝajnas al mi nek pli gajiga nek pli fruktodona ol la monteto mem. Sed ĉu oni volas kuŝigi nin tie ĉi ? certe de dek minutoj (or : de almenaŭ dek minutoj), ni restas sur tiu ĉi stacio.

Oni sendube atendas alian vagonaron, kiu devas pasi antaŭ la nia.

Mi kredas, ke efektive la rapida de Marseille (Marsej') atingas nin tie ĉi.

Sed kie ni haltos por matenmanĝi ?

Ni haltos en N   , la bufedo estas tie tre bona,
oni diris al mi.

Je kioma horo? ĉar mi tre vere mortas de
malsato.

Vi tamen vespermanĝis kiel manĝegulo hieraŭ
vespere.

Jes, sed de tiu tempo ni marŝadis.

Ho! marŝi tiamaniere ne estas tre lacige.

Vi estas prava, sed kiam oni ricevas skuadon kiel
ni dum ok horoj, oni digestas multe pli rapide.

Konsolu vin, nur unu duonon da horo vi nun
devas atendi.

Preparu (*or* tenu prete) vian bileton : mi ekvidas
la kontroliston.

Ankoraŭ! tiu homo malhelpos do al ni konstante.

Tiun ĉi fojon, ne plendu; tio estas la signo ke ni
atingas la celon.

Mi ne trovas mian kvitancon de pakaĵoj. Kion mi
faris el ĝi? Ha! jen ĝi estas.

Ĉu vi elektis hotelon?

Ne. Oni rekomendis al mi la hotelon de la Poŝto,
sed mi kredas ke ni agos pli saĝe, se ni decidos la
aferon tiam nur, kiam ni estos mem esplorintaj. Ni
prenu veturilon kaj lasu la pakaĵojn en la stacidomo.

Ha! jen estas hotelo kiu ŝajnas al mi sufiĉe pura.
Ĉu vi volas ke ni haltigu la veturilon?

Jes, ni malsupreniru.

Bonan tagon, sinjorino. Ĉu vi povus luigi al ni
ĉambron?

Certe, sinjoroj, kun plezuro (*or* plezure). Mi tuj
montros al vi tre belan ĉambron kun du litoj, aŭ, se
vi preferos, du ĉambrojn apartajn.

Jes, du ĉambrojn apartajn sed komunikiĝajn.

Ĉu vi deziras ilin kun vido sur la placon aŭ kun
vido sur la korton internan de la hotelo? Kompreneble
tiuj ĉi lastaj estas malpli karaj ol la aliaj.

Ĉar ni estos en la ĉambro nur nokte, la flanko sur

G 2

la korto sufiĉos al ni. Sed estu modera kaj ne tondu nin tro multe.

Ho! sinjoro, kion vi diras! Mi estas la plej modera el ĉiuj hotelistinoj.

Ĉi tiu ĉambro tre plaĉus al mi, se ĝi havus kabineton por la tualeto.˙

Mi havas alian tute similan, kiu plenumas tiun kondiĉon, sed ĝi estas iom malpli hela.

Tio ne ĝenas min. Montru ĝin al mi.

Jen ĝi estas, sinjoro. Ni povus loĝigi vian amikon en la apuda, kiu havas meblaron tute novan, kiel vi vidas.

Nu, tiuj du ĉambroj konvenas por ni. Je kia prezo vi luigas ilin?

Tio ĉi dependos de la tempo kiun vi pasigos tie ĉi, sinjoroj.

Se vi ne estos tro postulema, ni restos unu monaton, ĉar ni volas esplori tute bone la arbaron kaj la ĉirkaŭaĵojn.

Nu! vi pagos 12 frankojn ĉiu, por unu tago, se vi prenos la nutraĵon en la hotelo, kaj 7 frankojn, se vi ne manĝos tie ĉi.

Sed ĉu la lumo kaj la servado estas kalkulitaj en tiu prezo?

Jes, 12 frankojn por ĉiu tago. kalkulante ĉion, kun matenmanĝo, tagmanĝo kaj vespermanĝo. Sed ĉar la trinkaĵo de la lando estas cidro, se vi volos vinon, vi ĝin pagos aparte.

Bone; ni konsentas. Havu la bonecon prenigi niajn pakaĵojn el la stacidomo. Dume ni faros promeneton en la urbo.

VIZITO.

Mi pensas ke oni sonoris. Johano, iru do kaj vidu kiu estas tie. De neniu mi volas akcepti viziton hodiaŭ.

Sinjorino, ĝi estas sinjoro F . . . kiu insistas por esti akceptata. Mi diris al li ke la sinjorino estas suferanta ; sed li volas absolute ke mi avertu vin ke li havas tre gravan komunikon por fari al vi.

Nu ! respondu al li ke mi tre bedaŭras, sed ke mi estas vere tro malsaneta por akcepti lin. Kun tiu ĉi babilulo mi estus malhelpata du horojn.

Bone, sinjorino, mi tuj al li diros tion ĉi.

Nu ! ankoraŭ ekbato de sonorileto. Oni do ne lasos min trankvila. Kiu kredeble venas ankoraŭ min ĝeni ?

Ha ! ĝi estas sinjorino B . . . Johano diru al ŝi ke ŝi eniru kaj enkonduku ŝin en la saloneton.

Bonan tagon, kara amikino. Kiel vi sanas en tiu vetero peza kaj sufokiga, kiun ni havas de du tagoj. Oni pensus ke oni estas en Senegalo.

Mi sanas tre bone, dankon. Prezentu al vi ke mi benas ĝuste tiun ĉi temperaturon, pri kiu ĉiuj plendas, ĉar mi bone esperas ke ĝi baldaŭ liberigos min de forta malvarmumo, kiu min tenas de mia reveno el Parizo.

Kaj kie ĝi kaptis vin ?

Ĉu iam oni scias kie malvarmumo kaptas iun ? Mi tamen kredas ke tio okazis al mi en la teatro. Al mi estis tre varme kaj elirante mi ne sufiĉe kovris min.

Oni neniam estas sufiĉe singarda. Sed kun tia vetero vi estos baldaŭ resanigita.

Mi jam venis por vin viziti ; sed mi pensas ke neniu estis ĉe vi, ĉar mi sonoris, mi frapis la pordon almenaŭ dek fojojn, ne atingante ke oni malfermu al mi.

Kiun tagon vi venis ?

Tion ĉi mi ne memoras pli ĝuste. En la lasta lundo vespere, mi pensas.

Je kioma horo ?

Je la duono de la sesa (horo), se mi ne eraras.

Vi kredeble eraras, aŭ pri la tago, aŭ pri la horo.

Eble ; cetere tio ĉi estas ne grava, ĉar mi vidas vin hodiaŭ kaj en bona sano.

Ĉu vi bone amuzis vin en Parizo ?

Mi, ho ! grandege, sed mia edzo, kiu nun amas nur la kamparon, havis unu solan deziron : tien ĉi reveni kiel eble plej baldaŭ.

Kaj, komprenelle, por ne suferigi lin tro forte, vi revenis pli baldaŭ ol vi volis.

Jes, sed en la edzeco oni devas havi la kuraĝon fari oferaĵojn unu al la alia. Kaj vi, ĉu vi ne intencas vojaĝi tiun ĉi jaron ?

Jes, ni intencas iri al la bordo de la maro. Sed mi atendas ke mia filo estu elirinta el la kolegio.

Ĉu vi estas kontenta je li ?

Li estas bona knabo, kvieta, obea sed senenergia.

Vi estas eble tro postulema.

Ne, mi certigas al vi, sed vere li timas tro multe ĉiun penon.

Kreskante li fariĝos pli kuraĝa kaj pli laborema.

Nu ! kara amikino, mi vin lasas.

Kiel, vi jam foriras !

Jes, mi promesis ke mi estos reveninta je la kvina horo, kaj estas jam la duono de la sesa.

PART IV

LETTERS—COMMERCIAL, ETC.

Parizo, la 1ªⁿ de Sep., 1901ª.

Kara Sinjorino,

Mi skribis al vi hieraŭ, sed mia letero kruciĝis
kun la via. Mi tre volonte enskribigas vin inter la
membroj-adeptoj de nia societo. Mi esperas ke vi
faros ĉion kion vi povos por vastigi la karan lingvon
inter viaj amikoj.

Kun amika saluto,
Via,

Sinjorino C   D

Nov-Jorko, 3. 11. 1902ª.

Tre estimata Sinjoro,

Hodiaŭ mi ricevis la ekzempleron de du gazetoj,
kiujn vi, aminde, sendis al mi. Koran dankon!

Tre fidele la via,

Sinjoro P . . .   B

Jorko, 1902ª.

Kara Amiko,

Ĉiujn bondezirojn pri ĝoja Kristnasko kaj pri
feliĉo kaj progreso en ĉiuj bonaĵoj en la nova jaro!

Kun kora saluto,

Sinjoro F . . .   L

Berlino, 2^{an} de Nov., 1901ᵃ.

Kara Sinjoro,

Mi resendis la artikolon kun traduko al la jurnalo per la poŝto foriranta je 11.30 matene, kaj esperas ke ĝi alvenos ne tro malfrue por aperi morgaŭ. Mi ankoraŭ ne scias detalojn pri la fondo de la nova societo.

Kore via,

Sinjoro D   V

Londono, 15^{an} de Jan., 1901ᵃ.

Estimata Sinjoro,

Mi volus vin viziti lundon, je la kvara horo post tagmezo, se tiu horo estus konvena al vi. Se mi ne ricevus respondon, mi estus ĉe vi je la horo nomita.

Kun saluto,

Sinjoro M   N . .

Dublino, 10^{an} de Junio, 1901ᵃ.

Kara Sinjoro,

Mi treege deziras havi pruvon de la praktikeco de "Esperanto." Ĉu vi volas korespondadi kun mi per poŝtkartoj ilustritaj ? Per tiuj ĉi ni povus doni reciproke kelkajn detalojn pri la diversaj vidaĵoj de niaj du landoj.

Kun kora saluto,

Sinjoro F . . .   O

Madrido, 26^{an} de Novembro, 1902ᵃ

Estimata Samideano,

Permesu al mi prezenti mian gratulon pri via kurso. Mi tre ŝatas vian manieron skribi, ĉiam uzante la estintan tempon de la verbo anstataŭ la estonta. Sendu al mi klarigojn pri via kurso Esperanta. Kie estas la kunveno, kiam ĝi fariĝas, kiu estas ĝia instruisto, kiom da lernantoj vi havas, k.c.

Sendu al nia gazeto artikolojn aŭ detalojn pri Esperanto, ni bezonas iom da ili. Mi petegas vin uzi nian gazeton kiel vian propran. Mi enmetos ĉion, kion vi sendos, ĉu Angla aŭ Esperanto.

Tute via,

Sinjoro X . . .   V . .

Lisabono, 3^{an} de Oktobro, 1902^a.

Kara Sinjoro,

Mi sciiĝis de S⁰ L. Marko ke vi interesiĝas je la lingvo Esperanto. Mi esperas ke vi helpos en la disvastigado de la kara lingvo en tiu ĉi lando, kie novaj aferoj ne estas akceptataj rapide.

Eble vi legis la bonan raporton pri Esperanto en la artikolo farita de S⁰ W. T. Stead en la "Revuo de Revuoj" por tiu ĉi monato

Kun frata respekto,

Sinjoro B . . .   A

Berlino, 9^{an} de Oktobro, 1901^a.

Kara Sinjoro,

Mi ricevis vian leteron de la 10^a de la kuranta monato kun viaj proponoj pri liveroj kaj la anonco pri viaj specimenoj, kiuj ankaŭ bone alvenis. En aliaj cirkonstancoj, estus malfacile por mi, ĉar mi ne havas motivojn por forlasi miajn kutimajn liverantojn, kiuj kontentigas min. Tamen, ĉar la prezoj kiujn vi prezentas al mi estas iom pli malkaraj, mi mendas de vi, por provo, cent rismojn da papero konforma je la specimeno No. 1, kaj tiom same da No. 2.

Se viaj liveroj estos kontentigaj, kiel mi esperas, mi sendos al vi pli grandajn mendojn.

Por la pago, volu prezentigi kambion al mia

kontoro, post tridek tagoj, kun 2 % da diskonto, konforme je viaj kondiĉoj.

Koncerne vian proponon pri drapoj, mi bedaŭras ke mi ne povas profiti ĝin, ĉar mi tute min ne okupas je tiuj komercaĵoj.

Atendante vian avizon pri la sendo, mi prezentas al vi, Sinjoro, mian sinceran saluton.

Sinjoro P. Grandaire en Lyon.   J. L.

C   la 2^{an} de Nov., 1901ª

Sinjoroj,

Ricevinte vian sendaĵon mi devas kun bedaŭro sciigi al vi, ke mi ne trovis ĉiun oleon eteran en kvalito tia, kian mi deziris kaj kian mi povas bezoni. Precipe mi trovis la oleon mentan, koncerne purecon, tiel malbonkvalita, ke ĝia valoro estas tre pli malalta ol la ordinara.

Ĉar la nomita oleo ŝajnis al mi suspektinda, mi decidis fari al ĝi pli zorgan ĥemian analizon, kaj jen mi trovis, entreprenante la sulfuracidan alkoholprovon de Hager, ke la oleo estas falsigita per oleo sasafrasa !

Ĉar mi do tian ne povas uzi, mi estas devigita resendi ĝin al vi kaj mi petas samtempe pri tuja nova sendaĵo da pura oleo, ĉar alie mi devos tiun saman aliloke prizorgi.

Atendante vian baldaŭan respondon, mi estas kun estimo.

Via,

Sinjoroj N. N.   O. O.

Amsterdamo, la 3^{an} de Februaro, 1902ª.

Sinjoro,

Vian estimatan adreson ni dankas al niaj komunaj amikoj sinjoroj N. N. kaj per tio ĉi ni permesas al ni proponi al vi niajn servojn por vendado kaj aĉetado de . sur tiu ĉi loko.

Ni multe ĝojos, se la nuna letero estos la komenco por korespondado, kiu povas esti utila tiel al vi kiel al ni, kaj ni vin certigas ke en ĉiu okazo ni penos fari ĉion eblan por la interesoj de niaj estimataj klientoj.

Donante la referencojn sube skribitajn, ni estas pretaj laŭ via deziro sendi al vi niajn kondiĉojn la plej malaltajn kaj ni atendas vian afablan respondon.

Kun alta estimo,

Referencoj :   N. N.
Sinjoroj N. N.

Parizo, la 5^{an} de Aprilo, 1903^a.

Gesinjoroj!

Ni havas la honoron sciigi al la Estimindaj Legantoj de " Korrespondens" ke ni posedas la literojn specialajn por presi Esperanton, kaj ke ni estas tute aranĝtaj por la preso de ĉiuj Leteroj, Cirkuleroj, Broŝuroj, Revuoj, k. t. p. kiujn ili povus bezoni.

Tiujn ni ĉiam presos tre zorge kaj kiel eble plej malkare.

Volu akcepti, Gesinjoroj, nian sinceran saluton.

S. S.

Londono, la 4^{an} de Januaro, 1901^a.

Estimata Sinjoro,

Kiel Esperantisto, permesu ke mi petu de vi la sekvantan servon.

Sinjoro B... el X... posedas ŝipon nomatan Olga, kiu nun prenas ŝarĝon en New-York por tiu ĉi haveno, kaj mi skribas al li hodiaŭ por proponi mian servon kiel ŝipa makleristo.

Ĉar li kredeble ne konas eĉ mian nomon, ĉu vi kompleze volus rekomendi min al tiu Sinjoro? Vi povus certigi lin, ke mi tre zorge min okupus je la aferoj de lia ŝipo.

Kun mia antaŭa danko, volu akcepti tre sinceran saluton de

via,

Sinjoro A . . .   B

Berlino, la 8^{an} de Januaro, 1901^a.

Estimata Sinjoro,

Mi ricevis vian leteron de la 4^a de tiu ĉi monato kaj volonte plenigus vian deziron parolante pri vi al sinjoro B . . . ; bedaŭrinde mi konas lin tro malmulte, por ke mia rekomendo povu esti efika. Mi do transdonis vian leteron al unu amiko mia, kiu havas pli oftajn rilatojn kun tiu sinjoro, kaj mi esperas, ke per li vi atingos la deziratan celon.

Ĉiam preta por servi al vi, mi restas,

tre via,

Sinjoro B   A

Nov-Jorko, la 9^{an} de Februaro, 1901^a

Estimata Sinjoro,

Mi ricevis ĝiatempe vian leteron de la 4^a de Marto, kaj mi renkontis hieraŭ sinjoron D., kiu varme rekomendis vin kaj petis, ke mi konfidu al vi la aferojn de mia ŝipo OLGA.

Ĉar mi havas ankoraŭ nenian agenton en via urbo, mi estas preta akcepti vian proponon ; sed mi antaŭe deziras, ke vi konigu al mi vian plej moderan prezon por la ricevo kaj ekspedo de la dirita ŝipo.

Se viaj kondiĉoj estas akcepteblaj kaj se mi estos kontentigita de via servo, mi volonte adresos al vi ĉiujn pluajn ŝipojn, kiujn mi poste sendos al via haveno.

Atendante vian baldaŭan respondon, mi subskribas, kun estimo.

Sinjoro C .   D . .

Parizo, la 2^{an} de Junio, 1902^a.

Estimata Sinjoro,

Aŭdinte ke vi nun havas lokon liberan en via oficejo, mi per tiu ĉi letero venas, kun la rekomendo de S⁰ E . . . , proponi al vi mian servon, kaj esperas, ke vi favore akceptos ĝin.

Mi estas dudekjara kaj estis jam dum tri jaroj komizo en la firmo F . . . kaj K⁰, kies almetita atesto montros al vi, ke ili ĉiam estis kontentigataj de miaj servoj kaj ke mi ilin forlasis laŭ propra volo, por serĉi pli profitan situacion. Krom Esperanto mi scias la lingvojn anglan kaj germanan; mi ankaŭ konas la librotenadon kaj stenografion.

Atendante la honoron ricevi vian respondon, mi prezentas al vi, Sinjoro, mian respektan saluton.

Sinjoro N . . .   E . . .

Londono, 6^{an} de Junio, 1902^a.

Estimata Sinjoro,

Mi permesas al mi sciigi vin, ke mia reprezentanto S⁰ G. en la nuna monato havos la honoron prezenti sin ĉe vi, por proponi diversajn komercaĵojn, kiujn mi povas nun liveri en kondiĉoj vere profitaj.

Mi esperas, ke vi lin akceptos kun via kutima afableco kaj ke vi donos al li kelkajn mendojn, kiujn mi promesas plenumi akurate kaj kontentige.

Kiel ĉiam al viaj ordonoj, mi restas,

Tre sincere via,

Sinjoro O . . .   M . .

Parizo, en la 15^{an} de Februaro, 1902^a.

Al sinjoroj H. Eriksen kaj K⁰· Kristiania.

Sinjoroj,

Mi legis en la gazeto Korrespondeus ke vi deziras kontoriston, kiu, krom librokonduko, komprenas la francan lingvon kaj la lingvon internacian Esperanto.

Mi posedas la deziratajn sciojn, kaj tial mi permesas al mi proponi al vi mian servadon por la vakanta loko (okupado).

En la tempo de tri jaroj mi estis okupata en la instituto de komercinstruisto, direktoro Hermod. Sinjoro Hermod donos al vi ĉiujn informojn, kiujn iel vi deziras tuŝante mian konduton kaj taŭgecon. Cetere mi vin certigas, ke mi penados meriti vian kontenton per ĝusta plenumado de miaj devoj.

Atendante vian bonvolan respondon, mi havas la honoron esti

Via humila servanto,

P

Bombe'o, 6^{an} Februaron, 1903ª.

Al S-roj Scott & Mc.Dowell, Glasgo.

Karaj Sinjoroj,

Konfirmante nian leteron datitan 17^{an} lastan monaton, ni petas vin nun akcepti al scio ke ni subskribis kontraŭ vi, per la ordono kaj por la kalkulo de S-roj Lapis Fratoj, Milano, unu kambion laŭ la sekvantaj detaloj :—No. 789. £321 : 10 : 0. Post 3 monatoj. Ordono :—Grindley & May.

Ni enmetas unu kopion de la fakturo pri la komercaĵoj enŝipigitaj pri kiuj ni subskribis la kambion : dua kaj tria kopioj sekvos per la plej proksima poŝto.

Rekomendante nian kambion al via atento, ni estas,

Viaj

LAW & ROE.

Lyon la 10^{an} de Marto, 1902ª.

Sinjoro,

Kun la rekomendo de honorinda negocisto de via regiono, mi permesas al mi adresi al vi mian prezaron ĝeneralan kaj samtempe kelkajn specimenojn de la vendobjektoj paperaj kaj kartonaj, kiujn mi havas ordinare en mia magazeno. Mi esperas ke vi ŝatos la kvaliton tute rimarkindan de la komercaĵoj kiujn mi proponas al vi, kaj ke la kondiĉoj profitaj, je kiuj mi povas liveri ilin al vi, decidigos vin doni al mi viajn mendojn.

Vi povas ankaŭ vidi en mia katalogo, ke, krom la paperoj, mi ankaŭ makleras pri ĉiuj komercaĵoj de la urbo Roubaix, speciale pri drapoj kaj teksaĵoj ĉiuspecaj. Miaj malnovaj kaj konstantaj interrilatoj kun ĉiuj firmoj ĉitieaj donas al mi la eblon trakti la negocojn de miaj mendantoj kun la tuta kompetenteco dezirinda kaj per tia maniero, ke ili estu plene kontentaj.

Esperante ke vi favoros min per viaj mendoj, mi petas, Sinjoro, ke vi akceptu mian sinceran saluton.

Sinjoro J.   P.

A FEW IDIOMATIC PHRASES.

1. *Mi skribos leteron hodiaŭ.*

1. I shall (write or am going to write) a letter to-day.

2. *Mi jus estis vidita de mia patro, aŭ, Mia patro jus min vidis.*

2. I have been seen just now by my father, or, My father saw me just now.

3. *Li estis jus pafota, sed oni lin pardonis.*

3. He was about to be shot, but they pardoned him.

4. *Mi estos devigata viziti (aŭ inviti) la doktoron morgaŭ.*

4. I am obliged to visit (or receive—see) the doctor to-morrow.

5. *Mi devos viziti la doktoron morgaŭ, aŭ, Estas necese ke mi vizitu, k.c.*

5. I have to visit (to see) the doctor to-morrow, or, It is necessary that I see, etc.

6. *Mi devas k.c.* (as in No. 5), *aŭ, Estas aranĝite ke mi vizitu, k.c.*

6. I am to see the doctor, etc., or, It is arranged that I am to see, etc.

7. *Estas necese ke mi vizitu la doktoron morgaŭ, aŭ, Mi efektive devas vidi (aŭ viziti) la doktoron, k.c.*

7. I must see the doctor, etc., or, In fact, I shall be obliged to see the doctor, etc.

8. *Mi deviĝis skribi leteron,*

8. I have been obliged to write a letter.

9. *Mi devis skribi leteron, aŭ, Estis necese ke mi skribu, k.c.*

9. I have had to write a letter, or, It was necessary that I write a letter.

10. *Mi sendube legis (aŭ tralegis) la libron, Mi pensas ke mi certe legis, k.c.*

10. I must have read the book, I think that I certainly read the book.

11. *Mi volas ricevi la sinjoron, Mi deziras ricevi, k.c., Mi estas preta por ricevi, k.c.*

11. I am willing to receive the gentleman. (The different translations must depend on context, and whether mere consent or desire is meant).

12. *Mi estis volanta ricevi la sinjoron, sed io okazis por ŝanĝi (aŭ ŝanĝante) mian volon, sed nun mi ne deziras lin ricevi.*

12. I was (have been) willing to receive the gentleman, but something happened to change my mind, or, but now I do not desire to receive him.

13. *Mi povas vidi la ŝipojn en la haveno, aŭ, Mi havas la povon vidi, k.c.*

13. I am able (can) see the ships in the harbor, or, I have the power to see, etc.

14 *Mi povus vidi la ŝipojn en la haveno, se mi estus posedinta bonan lornon.*

15. *Mi povis vidi la ŝipojn en la haveno.*

16. *Mi devas skribi, sed la tempo mankas.*

17. *Mi devis skribi, sed mi tute forgesis ĝin fari.*

18. *Mi jus estis skribonta, kiam la telegramo alvenis.*

14. I could have seen the ships in the harbor if I had had a good glass.

15. I was able (have been able) to see the ships in the harbor.

16. I ought to write, but I have no time (time is wanting).

17. I ought to have written, but I quite forgot to do it.

18. I was just about to write, when the telegram arrived.

PART V.—VOCABULARIES.

I.—ENGLISH-ESPERANTO.

The words contained in this vocabulary are quite sufficient for all ordinary purposes. I wish, however, to give the reader a few hints regarding the manner of using, in the event of his requiring any word not found in it.

1st. The word you look for may be perhaps a word common to most countries. For instance, you will not find such universal words as microphone, telephone, etc. In this case refer to the section on "Foreign words," and you will have no difficulty in forming such words for yourself.

2nd. The word you may want is perhaps a synonym, and this synonymous word you will, in all likelihood, find in the vocabulary. For instance, you may be looking for the verb "to seize"; if you cannot find it, look for the verb "to catch," etc.

3rd. Also if you want to find the word "short," look for its opposite "long" and prefix "Mal," and then you have it. The same way with scores, nay hundreds of other words. Hence it is well to have a good *working* knowledge of the prefixes and affixes. A thorough acquaintance with these will place almost every possible word within your reach. With a much briefer vocabulary than the one before you, I, by adopting these few rules, read everything I came across in Esperanto, and wrote all my correspondence with a large number of Esperantists.

4th. The words marked with an asterisk are invariable; the other words form different parts of speech by changing final letter, as *Ami*, to love (verb); *Amo*, love (noun); *Ame*, lovingly (adverb); *Ama*, loving (adjective).

A.

able kapabla.
about *pri, *ĉirkaŭ.
above *super.
accent akcento.
accompany akompani.
according to *laŭ.
account kalkulo.
accurate akurata.
accustom kutimi.
acid acido
acorn glano.
acquire akiri.
across *trans.
act agi.
actual efektiva.
add aldoni.
address adresi.
adept adepto.
adieu *adiaŭ.
administrate administri.
admire admiri.
adore adori.
advertise anonci.
affair afero.
after *post.
again re.
against *kontraŭ.
age aĝo.
agreeable agrabla.
agree konsenti.
ah ! *ha.
aim celi.
air (subst.) aero.
air (vb.) aerumi.

album albumo.
alder alno.
all *ĉio, *ĉiuj.
allow permesi.
almond migdalo.
almost *preskaŭ.
alms almozo.
alone sola.
alphabet alfabeto.
already *jam.
also *ankaŭ.
although *kvankam.
always *ĉiam.
ambassador ambasadoro.
amber sukceno.
among *inter.
amuse amuzi.
anchor ankro.
ancient antikva
and *kaj.
angel anĝelo.
anger kolero.
angle angulo.
annoy enui.
answer respondi.
ant formiko.
anxiety maltrankvilo.
any *ia.
anyhow *iel.
anyone *iu.
anyone's *ies.
anything *io.
anytime *iam.
anywhere *ie.
appear aperi.
apple pomo.
apricot abrikoto.

arbor laŭbo.
arch arko.
argue disputi.
argument argumento.
arm brako.
around *ĉirkaŭ.
arouse veki.
arrange aranĝi.
arrow sago.
arsenic arseniko.
art arto.
artichoke artiŝoko.
as *kiel.
ash cindro.
ash-tree frakseno.
ask demandi.
asparagus asparago.
ass azeno.
assist helpi.
at *en, *ĉe, *apud.
at least *almenaŭ.
attack ataki.
attain atingi.
attempt provi.
attentive atenta.
attest atesti.
author aŭtoro.
authority rajto.
average mezonombro.
avoid eviti.
await atendi.
awake veki.
away *for.
axis akso.
azote [nitrogen] azoto.

B.

bachelor fraŭlo.
back (subst.) dorso.
badger melo.
bag sako.
baggage pakaĵo.
bake baki.
balance balanci.
ball pilko.
bank banko.
baptize bapti.
bar bari.
bare nuda.
bark [of dog] bojo.
bark [of tree] ŝelo.
barley hordeo
barrel barelo.
basket korbo.
bat vesperto.
bath banilo.
battle batalo.
be esti.
beak beko.
beam [of sun] radio.
beam [of wood] trabo.
bean fabo.
bear (subst.) urso.
bear (vb.) porti, toleri.
bear (to produce) produkti.
beard barbo.
beast besto.
beat bati.
beautiful bela.
beaver kastoro.
become fariĝi.
bed lito.

bed [garden] bedo.
bee abelo.
beech fago.
beer biero.
beet beto.
beetle skarabo.
before *antaŭ.
beg peti.
begin komenci.
behind *post.
behold rigardi
believe kredi.
belly ventro.
belong aparteni.
bench benko.
bend (v. a.) fleksi.
bend (v. n.) klini.
beneath *sub.
berry bero.
beside *preter, *ekster.
bet veti.
betroth fianĉigi.
between *inter.
bicycle biciklo.
bilberry mirtelo.
bind ligi.
bind [books] bindi.
bird birdo.
birch betulo.
biscuit biskvito.
bite mordi.
black nigra.
bladder veziko.
blame mallaŭdi.
bleat bleki.
bless beni.
blind (adj.) blinda.

blood sango.
blow (vb.) blovi.
blue blua.
body korpo.
boil (vb.) boli.
bolt riglo.
bone osto.
bonnet ĉapelo.
book libro.
book-keeping librotenado.
boot boto.
bore (vb.) bori.
borrow prunte preni.
both *ambaŭ.
bottle botelo.
bottom fundo.
boundary limo.
bouquet bukedo.
bourse borso.
bow [to shoot with] arko.
bow [of fiddle] arĉo.
bowl kaliko.
box (subst.) kesto.
box (vb.) bati, pugni.
boy knabo.
brain cerbo.
branch branĉo.
brandy brando.
bread pano.
break rompi.
bream bramo.
breast brusto.
breathe spiri.
brick briko.
bridge ponto.
bridle brido.

bright brila.
broad larĝa.
brother frato.
brown bruna.
brush broso.
bucket sitelo.
buckwheat poligono.
bud burĝono.
buffalo bubalo
buffet bufedo.
bug cimo.
build konstrui.
bulb bulbo.
bull bovo.
bullet kuglo.
bundle fasko.
bureau kontoro, oficejo.
burn (v. n.) bruli.
burn (v. a.) bruligi.
but *sed.
butter butero.
butterfly papilio.
button butono.
buy aĉeti.
by *per, *po, *apud.

C.

cabbage brasiko.
cabin kajuto.
cactus kakto.
cage kaĝo.
cake kuko.
calculate kalkuli.
calico kalikoto.
call voki.
camel kamelo.

can (subst.) kruĉo.
can (vb.) povas.
canary kanario.
candle kandelo.
candy kando.
cane kano.
capable kapabla.
car [railroad] vagono.
caraffe karafo.
card karto.
care zorgi.
caress karesi.
carp [fish] karpo.
carpenter ĉarpento.
carpet tapiŝo.
carriage kaleŝo.
carrot karoto.
case skatolo.
cash kaso.
cast [metals] fandi.
cast [throw] ĵeti.
castle kastelo.
cat kato.
catarrh kataro.
catch kapti.
caterpillar raŭpo.
cause kaŭzi.
cave kavo.
cavern kaverno.
cease ĉesi, halti.
cedar cedro.
ceiling plafono.
cellar kelo.
cement cemento.
certain certa.
chagrin ĉagreno.
chain ĉeno.

chalk kreto.
chamber ĉambro.
chamomile kamomilo.
change ŝanĝi.
chapter ĉapitro.
charm ĉarmi.
chase ĉasi.
chatter babili.
cheat trompi.
check vango.
cheese fromaĝo.
chemise ĉemizo.
chemistry ĥemio
cheque ĉeko.
cherish flegi.
cherry ĉerizo.
chess ŝakoj.
chestnut kaŝtano.
chew maĉi.
chief ĉefo.
child infano.
chin mentono.
chisel ĉizilo.
chocolate ĉokolado.
choose elekti.
cigar cigaro.
cigarette cigaredo.
cinder cindro.
circumstance cirkonstanco.
claim postuli.
clamp (bracket) krampo.
clay argilo.
clean pura.
clear klara.
clerk komizo.
clever lerta.
clock horloĝo.

cloth [a] tuko.
cloth [goods] drapo.
clothe vesti.
cloud nubo.
club klubo.
coal karbo.
coal-oil petrolo.
coast bordo.
cod gado.
coffee kafo.
coffin ĉerko.
collar kolumo.
collect kolekti.
color koloro.
column kolono.
comb kombi.
come veni.
comma komo.
command ordoni.
commerce komerco.
commission komisio.
committee komitato.
common komuna, ordinara.
communicate komuniki.
companion kolego.
compare kompari.
compassion kompato.
complain plendi.
conceal kaŝi.
concerning *pri.
conclude konkludi.
condition kondiĉo.
conduct konduto.
conduct (vb.) konduki.
confess konfesi.
confide konfidi.
confuse konfuzi.

congratulate gratuli.
conquer venki.
conscience konscienco.
conscious konscia.
consent konsenti.
console konsoli.
constant konstanta.
construct konstrui.
consumption ftizo.
content kontenta.
continue daŭri.
contract kontrakti.
convenient oportuna.
convince konvinki.
cook kuiri.
copper kupro.
copy kopio.
cork korko.
corn greno.
corn [on foot] kalo.
corner angulo.
correct korekti.
correspond korespondi.
cost kosti.
cotton kotono.
cough tusi.
count kalkuli.
counter kontoro.
country lando.
cousin kuzo.
cover kovri.
covetous avara.
crab kankro.
crafty ruza.
crane sarĝlevilo.
crane [bird] gruo.
cravat kravato.

crawl rampi.
cream kremo.
create krei.
cricket [insect] grilo.
crime krimo.
cross (subst.) kruco.
crowd amaso.
crown kroni.
cruel kruela.
crumple ĉifi.
cry krii.
cry [of beasts] bleki.
cuckoo kukolo.
cucumber kukumo.
cuff manumo.
cup taso.
cupboard ŝranko.
currant ribo.
curtain kurteno.
curved kurba.
cushion kuseno.
custom kutimo.
cut tranĉi.

D.

damage difekto.
dance danci.
danger danĝero.
date [fruit] daktilo.
day tago.
deaf, surda.
dear kara.
deceive trompi.
decide decidi.
deck ferdeko.

decree dekreto.
dedicate dediĉi.
deep profunda.
deer cervo.
defend defendi.
define difini.
deformed kripla.
demand postuli.
denounce denunci.
dense densa.
department departemento.
depict pentri, figuri.
desert dezerto.
desert forlasi.
deserve meriti.
design desegni.
desire deziri.
destroy detrui.
detail detalo.
devil diablo.
dew roso.
diameter diametro.
diamond diamanto.
die morti.
dig fosi.
diligent diligenta.
direct direkti.
disappoint ĉagreni
discharge [pour out] ŝuti.
discount diskonto, rabato.
dish plado.
dispute disputi.
distract distri.
distribution disdono.
diverse diversa.
divide dividi.
divine (vb.) diveni.

do fari.
dog hundo.
dollar dolaro.
doll pupo.
door pordo.
dot punkto.
doubt dubi.
dough pasto.
dove kolombo.
down (subst.) lanugo.
draw [out] tiri.
draw [along] treni.
draw [pictures] pentri.
drawers [chest of] komodo.
dream sonĝi.
drink trinki.
drop guti.
drown droni.
drug drogo.
drum tamburo.
dry seka.
duck anaso.
dumb muta.
dust polvo.
duty devo.

E.

each *ĉia, *ĉiu.
eagle aglo.
ear orelo.
ear [of grain] spiko.
early frua.
earth tero.
east oriento.

Easter pasko.
easy facila.
eat manĝi.
ecstasy ravo.
edge rando.
editor redaktoro.
educate eduki.
eel angilo.
effect efiki.
egg ovo.
eight *ok.
elastic elasta.
elbow kubuto.
elect elekti.
elephant elefanto.
elk alko.
embank digi.
embarrass ĝeni.
embrace ĉirkaŭpreni.
eminent eminenta.
enceinte graveda.
end fini.
endeavour peni.
endure daŭri.
engage okupi.
engineer inĝeniero.
eenugh sufiĉa.
entertain regali.
entice logi.
envelope koverto.
envy envio.
epoch epoko.
equal egala.
error eraro.
especially precipe.
establish fondi.
esteem estimi.

eternal eterna.
etiquette etiketo.
even (adj.) ebena.
even (adv.) *eĉ.
evening vespero.
every *ĉia
everyone *ĉiu.
everything *ĉio.
everywhere *ĉie.
examine ekzameni.
example ekzemplo.
except escepti.
exchange [bill of] kambio
execute ekzekuti.
exercise ekzerco.
exhibition ekspozicio.
exist ekzisti.
expedite ekspedi.
expel peli.
expend elspezi.
expert sperta.
explode eksplodi.
explore esplori.
express esprimi.
extinguish estingi.
extreme ekstrema.
eye okulo.
eyelid palpebro.

F.

fable fablo.
face vizaĝo.
fac-simile faksimilo.
fade velki.
faint sveni.

fair (subst.) foiro.
faithful fidela.
falcon falko.
fall [of *year*] aŭtuno.
fall (vb.) fali.
false falsa.
family familio.
fan ventumilo.
fancy revo.
fashion fasono.
fast (adj.) rapida.
fast (vb.) fasti.
fat grasa.
fate sorto.
father patro.
fathom klafto.
fault kulpo.
favor favori.
favor [do a] komplezi.
fear timi.
feast festi.
feel (v. a.) palpi.
feel (v. n.) senti.
felt felto.
fern filiko.
fever febro.
field kampo.
fig figo.
fight batali.
file fajlilo.
filter filtri.
find trovi.
finger fingro.
finish fini.
fir abio.
fire fajro.
fireplace fajrejo.

firm firma.
fish fiŝo.
fist pugno.
five *kvin.
flag standardo.
flat plata.
flatter flati.
flax lino.
fleece felo.
flint siliko.
flour faruno.
flow flui.
flower floro.
fluff lanugo.
fluid fluaĵo.
flute fluto.
fly (vb.) flugi.
fly (subst.) muŝo.
foam ŝaŭmo.
fog nebulo.
fold faldi.
follow sekvi.
foot piedo.
for *por, *pro, *ĉar.
forehead frunto.
foreign fremda.
forge forĝi.
forget forgesi.
forget-me-not miozoto.
forgive pardoni.
fork forko.
forth *for.
fortified fortika.
fortunate feliĉa.
fountain fonto.
four *kvar.
fox vulpo.

frame kadro.
franc franko.
free libera.
fresh freŝa.
Friday vendredo.
friend amiko.
fright teruro.
frog rano.
from *el, *de.
front fronto.
frost frosto.
fruit frukto.
frying pan pato.
fulfil plenumi.
full plena.
fume (subst.) haladzo.
funeral funebro.
fungus fungo.
fur pelto.
furious freneza.
furniture meblo.
furrow sulko.

G.

gain gajni.
gaiter gamaŝo.
gall galo.
garden ĝardeno.
garlic ajlo.
gas gaso.
gather kolekti.
gay gaja.
gentle ĝentila.
gentleman sinjoro.
genus gento.

get ricevi.
give doni, donaci.
glare heli.
glass vitro.
glass [a] glaso
globe globo.
glory gloro.
glove ganto
glue gluo.
gnat kulo.
go iri.
goat kapro.
God Dio.
gold oro.
good bona.
good-bye *adiaŭ.
goods ŝtofo.
goose ansero.
gooseberry groso.
grain greno.
grain [a] grajno.
grandfather avo.
grandson nepo.
grape vinbero.
grass herbo.
grasshopper akrido.
grease sebo.
great granda.
green verda.
grey griza.
grind mueli.
groan ĝemi.
grouse urogalo.
grow kreski.
gruel kaĉo.
guarantee garantio.
guard gardi.

guess diveni.
guest gasto.
gulf golfo.
gum gumo.
gunpowder pulvo.

H.

hail hajlo.
hair haro.
ham ŝinko.
hammer martelo.
hand mano.
handicraft metio.
handy lerta.
hang pendi.
hangings tapeto.
happen okazi.
happy feliĉa.
harbor haveno.
hardly *apenaŭ.
hare leporo.
harp harpo.
harrow erpi.
hat ĉapelo.
have havi.
hawk akcipitro.
hay fojno.
he li.
head kapo.
health sano.
hear aŭdi.
heart koro.
heat (v. a.) hejti.
heaven ĉielo.
heel kalkano.

hell infero.
helmet kasko.
help helpi.
hemp kanabo.
here *tie ĉi.
hero heroo.
heron ardeo.
herring haringo.
hew haki.
hide (subst.) haŭto.
hide (vb.) kaŝi.
high alta.
hinge ĉarniro.
hire dungi.
hit frapi.
hoarse raŭka.
hog porko.
hold teni.
hole truo.
holy sankta.
home hejmo.
honest honesta.
honey mielo.
honeysuckle lonicero.
honor honori.
hoof hufo.
hook hoko.
hope esperi.
hops lupolo.
horse ĉevalo.
horse-radish kreno.
host mastro.
hotel hotelo.
hour horo.
house domo.
how *kiel.
however *tamen, *do.

how much, many *kiom.
humble humila.
humming-bird kolibro.
humor humoro.
hump ĝibo.
hundred *cent.
hunt ĉasi.
hurt vundi.
husband edzo.

I.

I mi.
ice glacio.
if *se.
illustration ilustraĵo.
imitate imiti.
immediately *tuj.
important grava.
inch colo.
incite inciti.
incline klini.
increase kreski.
indeed *ja.
industrious diligenta.
industry industrio.
infant infano.
infect infekti.
influence influi.
inherit heredi.
injure vundi, difekti.
ink inko.
inner interna.
insect insekto.
insert enmeti.
instead *anstataŭ.
instruct instrui.
insult insulti.

insure asekuri.
intend intenci.
interest interesi.
intestine intesto.
invite inviti.
iron fero.
iron (vb.) gladi.
island insulo.
it ĝi.
itch juko.
ivy hedero.

J.

jacket jako.
jaw faŭko.
jealous ĵaluza.
jewel juvelo.
join jungi.
joint artiko.
joke ŝerci.
journal ĵurnalo.
journey veturo.
joy ĝojo.
jubilee jubileo.
judge juĝi.
jug kruĉo.
juice suko.
just (adj.) justa.
just (adv.) *ĵus.

K.

keep konservi.
keg barelo.
kernel kerno.
kerosene petrolo.

kettle kaldrono.
key ŝlosilo.
kidney reno.
kind (subst.) speco.
kind (adj.) aminda.
king reĝo.
kingdom regno.
kiss kisi.
knapsack tornistro.
knee genuo.
know scii, koni.

L.

labor labori.
lace pasamento.
lake lago.
lame lama.
land lando.
language lingvo.
lantern lanterno.
lard lardo.
large granda.
lark alaŭdo.
last (adj.) lasta.
last (vb.) daŭri.
laugh ridi.
law leĝo.
lead (subst.) plumbo.
lead (vb.) konduki.
leaf folio.
lean (vb.) apogi.
leap salti.
learn lerni.
leather ledo.
leave (subst.) permeso.

leave (vb.) lasi.
leech hirudo.
legend legendo.
legume legomo.
lemon citrono.
lend prunte doni.
lentil lento.
lesson leciono.
letter letero.
letter [of alphabet] litero.
lick leki.
lie [down] kuŝi.
lie [tell a] mensogi.
lift levi.
light (subst.) lumo.
lightning fulmo.
like (vb.) ŝati, ami.
like (adj.) simila.
lily lilio.
lime kalko.
limit limo.
line linio.
linen tolo.
lion leono.
lip lipo.
listen aŭskulti.
live vivi, loĝi.
liver hepato.
lizard lacerto.
lo ! *jen.
load [a gun] ŝargi.
lock (subst.) seruro.
lock (vb.) ŝlosi.
locomotive lokomotivo
lodge loĝi.
long (adj.) longa.
long (vb.) sopiri.

lose perdi.
lot [cast] loto.
lottery loterio.
loud laŭta.
lounge kanapo.
love ami.
lucifer alumeto.
lung pulmo.

M.

machine maŝino.
mad kolera, freneza.
magpie pigo.
mail poŝto.
maize maizo.
majesty majesto.
make fari.
man homo, viro.
manner maniero.
manufactory fabriko.
many multa.
maple acero.
marble marmoro.
margin marĝeno.
marsh marĉo.
mason masonisto.
mass amaso.
mast masto.
master mastro.
mat mato.
match alumeto.
mattress matraco.
meal faruno, manĝado.
means rimedo
measure mezuri.

meat viando.
medalion medaliono.
medicine kuracilo.
meet renkonti.
melon melono.
member membro.
memory memoro.
mercury hidrargo.
mesh maŝo.
miasma haladzo.
middle mezo.
migrate migri.
mile mejlo.
milk (subst.) **lakto.**
milk (vb.) **melki.**
mill mueli.
millet milio.
mind animo, cerbo.
mine mia (poss. pron.).
mirror spegulo.
misery mizero.
mix miksi.
mixture miksaĵo.
model modeli.
moderate modera.
modest modesta.
molasses siropo.
mole talpo.
Monday lundo.
money mono.
monk monaĥo.
monkey simio.
month monato.
moon luno.
more *pli.
morning mateno.
moss musko.

most *plej.
moth tineo.
mountain monto.
mourn plori.
mouse muso.
mouth buŝo.
move movi.
mow falĉi.
much multe.
mucilage gumo.
mud koto.
mulberry moruso.
mule mulo.
murmur murmuri.
mushroom fungo.
must (vb.) devis.
mustard mustardo.

N.

nail najlo.
nail [finger] ungo.
naked nuda.
name nomi.
nape nuko.
nation nacio.
nature naturo.
near proksima.
near to (prep.) *apud.
necessary necesa.
neck kolo.
need (vb.) bezoni.
neigh bleki.
neighbor najbaro.
neither *nek.
nephew nevo.
nest nesto.

net reto.
nettle urtiko.
never *neniam.
new nova.
night nokto.
nightingale najtingalo.
nine *naŭ.
no *ne.
noble nobla.
nobleman nobelo.
nobody *neniu.
nohow *neniel.
noise bruo.
none *neniom.
no one's *nenies.
nor *nek.
north nordo.
nose nazo.
not *ne.
nothing *nenio.
nourish nutri.
now *nun.
nowhere *nenie.
number nombro, numero.
nut nukso.

O.

oak kverko.
oar remilo.
oats aveno.
obey obei.
óbject objekto.
objéct kontraŭstari.
obstinate obstina.
obstruct bari.
occasion okazo.

occupy okupi.
odor odoro.
of *de, *da.
offend ofendi.
offer [sacrifice] oferi.
offer [present] prezenti.
officiate agi.
often ofte.
oh ! *ho.
oil oleo.
on *sur.
one *unu.
onion bulbo.
only (adj.) sola.
only (adv.) *nur.
opinion opinio.
opportune ĝustatempe.
opposite *kontraŭ.
or *aŭ.
orange oranĝo.
order (subst.) ordo.
order (vb.) ordoni.
ordinary ordinara.
organ orgeno.
oriental orienta.
ornament ornamo.
orphan orfo.
ostrich struto.
other alia.
ought devi.
out *for.
outside *ekster.
oval ovalo.
oven forno.
over *super.
overcoat surtuto, super-
vesto.

overthrow renversi.
owe ŝuldi.
owl strigo.
own (vb.) posedi.
own (adj.) propra.
ox bovo.
oyster ostro.

P.

pack paki.
page paĝo.
pail sitelo.
pain doloro.
paint pentri.
paint-brush peniko.
pale pala.
palace palaco.
palate palato.
pants pantalono.
paper papero.
paradise paradizo.
pardon pardoni.
parrot papago.
parsley petroselo.
part parto.
particularly precipe.
partridge perdriko.
pass pasi.
passion pasio.
pastor pastro.
pasture paŝto.
patch fliko.
patience pacienco.
pause halti.
pavement pavimo.

pay pagi.
pea pizo.
peace paco.
peach persiko.
peacock pavo.
pear piro.
pearl perlo.
pen plumo.
pencil krajono.
penny penco.
people popolo.
pepper pipro.
perceive rimarki.
perch [fish] perĉo.
perfect perfekta.
perish perei.
permit permesi.
persecute persekuti.
person persono.
perspire ŝviti.
perverse petola.
petticoat jupo.
pheasant fazano.
piano fortepiano.
pickle pekli.
piece peco.
pike [fish] ezoko.
pillar kolono.
pin pinglo.
pinch pinĉi.
pine pino.
pineapple ananaso.
pious pia.
pipe pipo.
pitch peĉo.
pity (vb.) bedaŭri.
pity [it is a] domaĝo.

place loko.
plague pesto.
plait plekti.
plane (vb.) raboti
plant (vb.) planti.
plant (subst.) kreskaĵo.
plate telero.
play ludi.
please plaĉi.
pleasure plezuro.
plenty sato.
plough (vb.) plugi.
plum pruno.
pocket poŝo.
point punkto.
poison veneno.
pole stango.
police polico.
polish poluri.
polish [for shoes] ciro.
poplar poplo.
poppy papavo.
porcelain porcelano.
possess posedi.
post [mail] poŝto.
pot poto.
pour verŝi.
powder (gun) pulvo.
powder (dust) pulvoro.
praise laŭdi.
pray preĝi.
preach prediki.
precise preciza.
prepare prepari.
present (subst.) donaco
present (vb.) prezenti.
preserve konservi.

press premi.
pretty beleta.
price kosto.
prick piki.
priest pastro.
prince princo
print presi.
private privata.
prize prezo.
produce produkti.
promise promesi.
proper propra.
property posedaĵo.
propose proponi.
prosper prosperi.
protect gardi, defendi.
proud fiera.
prove pruvi.
proverb proverbo.
prudent prudenta.
pull tiri.
pump pumpilo.
punish puni.
pure pura.
purple purpura.
pus puso.
push puŝi.
put meti.
puzzle enigmo.

Q,

quail koturno.
quality eco.
quantity kvanto.
quick rapida.

quicksilver hidrargo.
quiet trankvila.
quit lasi.

R,

rabbit kuniklo.
race gento.
radish rafano.
rag ĉifono.
rail relo.
railroad fervojo.
rain pluvi.
rake rasti.
rapid rapida.
raspberry frambo.
rat rato.
rate [at the — of] *po.
raven korvo.
ravish ravi.
ray [of sun] radio.
reach atingi.
read legi.
ready preta.
real efektiva.
reap rikolti.
receive ricevi.
recognise koni.
rectangle rektangulo.
red ruĝa.
regard rigardi.
regiment regimento.
register [a letter] reko-mendi.
reign regi.
rejoice ĝoji.

relate to rilati.
relation parenco.
remain resti.
remark rimarki.
remedy rimedo.
rent rento.
repeat ripeti.
repose ripozi.
represent figuri.
reproach riproĉi.
request peti.
require postuli.
resound sonori, resoni.
rest [the] cetero.
revenge venĝi.
reward rekompenci.
rhyme rimo.
rib ripo.
ribbon rubando.
rice rizo.
rich riĉa.
ride rajdi.
right [in the] prava.
right [authority] rajto.
right [hand] dekstra.
righteous justa.
ring ringo.
ripe matura.
river rivero.
road vojo.
roast rosti.
rob rabi.
roll ruli.
roof tegmento.
rook frugilego
room ĉambro.
rooster koko.

root radiko.
rope ŝnuro.
rose rozo.
rotten putra.
round ronda.
row [rank] vico.
row (vb.) remi.
rub froti.
rubber-shoe galoŝo.
rule regulo.
rum rumo.
run kuri.
rust rusti.
rye sekalo.

S.

sack sako.
sacrifice (v.) oferi.
sad malĝoja.
saddle selo.
sail velo.
salad salato.
salmon salmo.
salt salo.
salute saluti.
same sama.
sand sablo.
Saturday sabato.
sauce saŭco.
save savi.
saw segi.
say diri.
scale [fish, etc.] skvamo
scarcely *apenaŭ.
science scienco.
scissors tondilo.
scratch grati.

screw ŝraŭbo.
sculpture skulpti.
sea maro.
seagull mevo.
seal [animal] foko.
seal (vb.) sigeli.
search serĉi.
season sezono.
seat seĝi.
seductive deloga
see vidi.
seem ŝajni.
self si ; mem.
sell vendi.
send sendi.
sense senco.
separate aparta.
serpent serpento.
serve servi.
set [type] komposti.
seven *sep.
severe severa.
sew kudri.
shadow ombro.
shaft [of wagon, etc.] timono.
shake skui.
shame honto.
shark ŝarko.
sharp akra.
shave razi.
she *ŝi.
sheaf garbo.
shear tondi.
sheep ŝafo.
shell ŝelo, konko.
shield ŝildo.

shilling ŝilingo.
shine brili.
ship ŝipo.
shirt ĉemizo.
shoe ŝuo.
shoot pafi.
shore bordo.
short-sighted **miopa.**
shoulder ŝultro.
shovel ŝovelo.
show montri.
shut fermi.
side flanko.
sift kribri.
sign signo.
signify signifi.
silent silenta.
silk silko.
silver arĝento.
similar simila.
simple simpla.
sin peki.
sing kanti.
sir sinjoro.
sit sidi.
situation situacio.
six *ses.
skate gliti.
skilful lerta.
skin haŭto.
sleep dormi.
sleeve maniko.
slide gliti.
slippery glata.
smallpox variolo.
smear ŝmiri.
smell (subst.) odoro.

smell (vb.) flari.
smoke fumi.
smooth ebena, glata.
smoothe gladi.
snail limako
sneeze terni.
snow neĝo.
so *tiel.
soap sapo.
sober sobra.
society societo.
sofa kanapo, sofo.
soft mola.
sole [of foot] plando.
solve solvi.
some *ia, kelka, *iom.
somehow *iel.
someone *iu.
someone's *ies.
something *io.
sometime *iam.
somewhat *iom, *iel.
somewhere *ie.
so much *tiom.
son filo.
soon *baldaŭ.
soot fulgo.
sorcery sorĉo.
sorrow malĝojo.
soul animo.
sound soni.
soup supo.
south sudo.
sow semi.
sparrow pasero.
spawn frajo.
speak paroli.

special speciala.
spell silabi.
sphinx sfinkso.
spice spico.
spider araneo.
spin ŝpini.
spinach spinaco.
spirit spirito.
spit kraĉi.
spite [in—of] *malgraŭ.
spleen lieno.
split fendi.
sponge spongo.
spoon kulero.
spot makulo.
spring [time] printempo.
spring risorto.
sprinkle ŝpruci.
spur sprono.
square [public] placo.
squirrel sciuro
stable stalo.
stain makulo.
stairs ŝtuparo.
stammer balbuti.
stamp [metal, etc.] marko.
stamp [postage] poŝt-marko.
stand stari.
star stelo.
starch amelo.
starling sturno.
state stato.
station stacio.
steal ŝteli.
steam vaporo.
steel ŝtalo.

step ŝtupo.
stewpan kaserolo.
stick bastono.
still (adj.) kvieta.
still (adv.) *ankoraŭ.
sting piki.
stocking ŝtrumpo.
stomach stomako.
stone ŝtono.
stop ĉesi, halti.
stop up ŝtopi.
store magazeno.
stork cikonio.
story rakonto.
story [of house] etaĝo.
stove forno.
straight rekta.
strange stranga.
strap rimeno.
straw pajlo.
strawberry frago.
streak streko.
street strato.
stretch (v. a.) streĉi.
stride paŝo.
strike [hit] frapi.
string kordo (music).
strive peni.
strong forta.
stuff ŝtofo.
success sukceso.
such *tia.
suck suĉi.
sudden subita.
suffer suferi.
suffocate sufoki.
sugar sukero.

sulphur sulfuro.
summer somero.
sun suno.
Sunday dimanĉo.
supplement aldono.
support subapogi.
suppose supozi.
suspect suspekti.
suspenders ŝelko.
swallow [bird] hirundo
swallow (vb.) gluti.
swan cigno.
swear ĵuri.
sweep balai.
swell ŝveli.
swim naĝi.
swing svingi.
sword glavo.
syllable silabo.
sympathise kompati.

T.

table tablo.
tablet tabulo.
tail vosto.
tailor tajloro.
take preni.
tale fabelo
tall alta.
tallow sebo.
tap [water, etc.] krano.
tapestry tapeto.
tar gudro.
tassel glano.
taste gusti.
tax takso.

tea teo.
teach instrui.
tear larmo.
tear (vb.) ŝiri.
tedious teda.
telegraph telegrafi.
tell rakonti.
temple [of head] tempio.
ten *dek.
territory teritorio.
than *ol.
thank danki.
that (pron.) tiu ; tio.
that (conj.) *ke.
thaw degeli.
the *la, *l'.
the—the *ju—des.
theater teatro.
then *tiam.
there *tie.
therefore *tial.
they ili.
thick dika.
think pensi.
thirst soifo.
this *tiu ĉi.
thistle kardo.
though *kvankam.
thousand *mil.
thread fadeno.
threaten minaci.
three *tri.
thresh draŝi.
threshold sojlo.
thrift ŝparo.
throat gorĝo.
through *tra ; *per.

throw ĵeti.
thrush turdo.
thunder tondro.
Thursday ĵaŭdo.
thus *tiel.
ticket bileto.
tickle tikli.
tie ligi.
time tempo.
time(s) fojo.
tin stano.
tinplate lado.
tired laca.
to *al.
toad bufo.
today *hodiaŭ.
together *kune.
toilet tualeto.
tomb tombo.
tomorrow *morgaŭ.
tongue lango.
too *tro.
tooth dento.
torment turmenti.
tortoise testudo.
totter ŝanceli.
touch tuŝi.
towel viŝilo.
tower turo.
town urbo.
trade (subst.) komerco.
trade (vb.) komerci.
transact trakti.
translate traduki.
treaty kontrakto.
tree arbo.
tremble tremi.

triangle triangulo.
trouble zorgo.
true vera.
trumpet trumpeto.
trunk [of tree] trunko.
trust konfidi.
try provi.
tub barelo.
tube tubo.
Tuesday mardo.
tulip tulipo.
tune (subst.) melodio.
tune (vb.) agordi.
turkey meleagro.
turn turni.
turn [wood] torni.
turnip rapo.
twist (v. a) tordi.
twist (v. n.) volvi.
two *du.
type tipo.

U.

ulcer ulcero.
umbrella ombrelo.
uncle onklo.
under *sub.
understand kompreni.
undertake entrepreni.
until *ĝis.
upper supr.
upset renversi.
urge inciti.
use uzi.
useful utila.
utilise utiligi.

V.

vain vana.
valise valizo.
valley valo.
various diversa.
vase vazo.
vast vasta.
vein vejno.
velvet veluro.
verse verso.
vertical vertikala.
very *tre.
vest veŝto.
vignette vinjeto.
village vilaĝo.
vinegar vinagro.
violet violo.
violet (adj.) violkolora.
violin violono.
virtue virto.
visit viziti.
voice voĉo.
volcano vulkano.
volume volumo.
voyage vojaĝo.
vulture vulturo.

W.

wages salajro.
waist talio.
wait atendi.
walk promeni.
wall muro.
walnut juglando.

walrus rosmaro.
wander vagi.
want bezoni.
war milito.
warm varma.
wart veruko.
wash lavi.
wasp vespo.
water akvo.
wave ondo.
wax vakso.
way vojo.
we *ni.
weary laca, enua.
weather vetero.
weave teksi.
wedge kojno.
Wednesday merkredo.
week semajno.
weep plori.
weigh (v. a.) pesi.
weigh (v. n.) pezi.
well (subst.) puto.
west okcidento.
whale baleno.
what *kia, *kio.
wheat tritiko.
wheel rado.
when *kiam.
where *kie.
whether *ĉu.
while *dum.
whip vipo.
whistle fajfi.
white blanka
who *kiu.
whole tuta.

whose *kies.
why *kial.
wick meĉo.
wide larĝa, vasta.
widower vidvo.
wild sovaĝa.
will voli.
willow saliko.
wind (vb.) tordi.
wind (subst.) vento.
window fenestro.
wine vino.
wing flugilo.
winter vintro.
wipe viŝi.
wise saĝa.
wish deziri.
wit sprito.
with *kun.
within interne.
without (wanting) *sen.
without (outside) ekstere.
wolf lupo.
wonder miri.
wood (substance) *ligno*.
woodpecker pego.
wool lano.
word vorto.
work (manual) laboro.
work (mental) verko.
world mondo.
worm vermo.
wound vundi.
write skribi.

Y.

yawn oscedi.
year jaro.
yeast fermentilo.
yellow flava.
yes *jes.
yesterday *hieraŭ.
yet *ankoraŭ.
yoke jugo.
you vi.
young juna.

zenith zeni
zigzag zigz
zinc zinko.
zone zono.

A.

a termination of adjectives : *bel'o* beauty, *bel'a* beautiful.

abelo bee.

abio fir.

acero maple.

acida acid, sour.

aĉeti to buy.

ad' denotes duration of action : *danc'i* dance, *danc'ado* dancing.

adepto adept.

administri administrate.

adiaŭ adieu, good-by.

aero air.

afero affair, business.

aglo eagle.

agrabla agreeable.

aĝo age.

ajlo garlic.

ajn . . . ever : *kiu* who, *kiu ajn* whoever.

aj' made from or possessing the quality of : *sek'a* dry, *sek'ajo* dry goods.

akcento accent.

akcipitro hawk.

akompani accompany.

akra sharp.

akrido grass-hopper.

akurata accurate, punctual

akvo water.

al to.

alaŭdo lark (bird).

albumo album.

alia other.

alkovo alcove.

almenaŭ at least.

almozo alms.

alta high.

alumeto match (lucifer).

amo love.

amaso crowd, mass.

ambasadoro ambassador.

amelo starch.

amiko friend.

amuzi amuse.

an' inhabitant, member : *Nov-Jork'o* New York, *Nov-Jork'an'o* New Yorker.

anaso duck.

angulo corner, angle.

anĝelo angel.

animo soul.

ankaŭ also.

ankoraŭ yet, still.

ankro anchor.

anonci announce.

ansero goose.

anstataŭ instead of.

anta ending of pres. part. act. *in* verbs : *am'anta* loving.

antaŭ before.

aparti separate.

aparteni belong.

apenaŭ scarcely.

aperi appear.

apogi lean (vb.).

aprobo approbation.

apud near by.

ar' a collection of objects : *vort'o* word, *vort'aro* dictionary.

araneo spider.

aranĝi arrange.

arbo tree.

arĉo bow (fiddle).

ardeo heron.

argilo clay.

arĝento silver.

argumento argument.

arko arch, bow.

arseniko arsenic.

arto art.

artiko joint.

as ending of the present tense *in* verbs : *am'as* loves.

asparago asparagus.

ata ending of pres. part pass. in verbs : *am'ata* loved.

ataki attack.

atendi wait, expect.

atenti attend.

atesti attest, affirm.

atingi attain, reach.

aŭ or.

aŭdi hear.

aŭskulti listen.

aŭtuno fall (of the year).

avo grandfather.

avara covetous.

aveno oats.

azeno ass.

azoto azote, nitrogen.

B

babili chatter.

baki bake.

balai sweep.

balanci balance, swing.

balbuti stammer.

baldaŭ soon.

baleno whale.

bano bath.

bapti baptize.

bari bar, obstruct.

barbo beard.

barelo keg, barrel.

bastono stick.

bati beat.

batali fight.

bedo bed (garden).

bedaŭri pity, regret.

beko beak.

bela beautiful.

beni bless.

benko bench.
bero berry.
besto beast.
betulo birch (tree).
bezoni need, want.
biciklo bicycle.
bieno goods, estate.
biero beer.
bindi bind (books).
birdo bird.
blanka white.
bleki cry (of beasts).
blinda blind.
blovi blow.
blua blue.
bo' relation by marriage :
　patrino mother, bo'-
　patrino mother-in-law.
boli boil (vb. neut.).
boligi to boil (v. act.).
bona good.
bori bore (vb.).
bordo shore.
borso bourse, exchange.
boto boot.
botelo bottle.
bovo ox.
brako arm.
bramo bream.
branĉo branch.
brando brandy.
brasiko cabbage.
brido bridle.
briko brick.
brili shine.
brosi brush.
brovo eyebrow.

bruo noise.
bruli burn (v. n.).
bruna brown.
brusto breast.
bruto brute.
bufedo buffet.
bufo toad.
bulbo bulb.
burĝono bud.
buŝo mouth.
butero butter.
butono button.

C.

celi aim.
cent hundred.
cerbo brain.
certa certain, sure.
cervo deer.
cetero rest, remainder.
cifero cipher.
cigaro cigar.
cigaredo cigarette.
cigno swan.
cikonio stork.
cindro ash, cinder.
cirkonstanco circumstance.
citrono lemon.

Ĉ.

ĉagreni disappoint.
ĉambro chamber.
ĉapo bonnet, cap.
ĉapelo hat.
ĉapitro chapter.

ĉar for ; because.

ĉarmo charm.

ĉarniro hinge.

ĉarpenti do carpenter's work.

ĉasi hunt.

ĉe at, near, by.

ĉefo chief.

ĉeko cheque.

ĉemizo shirt.

ĉeno chain.

ĉerizo cherry.

ĉerko coffin.

ĉesi cease, desist.

ĉevalo horse.

ĉi denotes proximity : *tiu* that, *tiu ĉi* this ; *tie* there, *tie ĉi* here.

ĉia every.

ĉiam always.

ĉie everywhere.

ĉiel in every manner.

ĉielo heaven.

ĉifi crumple.

ĉifono rag.

ĉikano chicanery.

ĉio everything.

ĉirkaŭ about, around.

ĉiu each, every one, *ĉiu'j* all.

ĉizi chisel.

ĉj' affectionate diminutive of masculine names : *Johano* John, *Jo'ĉjo* Johnnie.

ĉokolado chocolate.

ĉu whether ; asks a question.

D.

da is used instead of *de* after words expressing weight or measure ; *funto da viando* a pound of meat, *taso da teo* a cup of tea.

daktilo date (fruit).

danci dance.

danĝero danger.

danki thank.

dato date (time).

daŭri endure, last.

de of, from.

decidi decide.

deĉifri decipher.

dediĉi dedicate.

defendi defend.

degradi degrade.

dek ten.

dekreto decree.

dekstro right-hand.

demandi demand, ask.

densa dense.

dento tooth.

denunci denounce.

des the (*ju . . . des* the the).

desegni design, draw.

detalo detail.

detrui destroy.

devi ought, must, *dev'igi* necessitate, compel.

dezerto desert.

deziri desire.

Dio God.

diamanto diamond.
diametro diameter.
difekti damage, injure.
diferenci distinguish.
difini define.
digesti digest.
digi embank.
dika thick.
dikti dictate.
diligenta diligent.
dimanĉo Sunday.
diri say.
direkti direct.
dis' has the same force as the English prefix *dis*—: *semi* sow, *dis'semi* disseminate ; *ŝiri* tear, *dis'ŝiri* tear to pieces.
disputi dispute.
distingi distinguish.
distri distract.
diveni divine, guess.
diversa various, diverse.
dividi divide.
do then, indeed, however.
dolaro dollar.
dolĉa sweet.
doloro pain, ache.
domo house.
domaĝo pity (in the phrase, it is a pity).
doni give, *al'doni* add.
donaci make a present.
dormi sleep.
dorso (the) back (of the body).
drapo woollen goods.

drapiri drape.
draŝi thresh.
droni drown
du two.
dubi doubt.
dum while, during, *dum'e* meanwhile.
dungi hire.

E.

e ending of adverbs *bon'a* good, *bon'e* well.
ebena even, smooth.
eble perhaps.
ec' denotes qualities ; *bon'a* good, *bon'eco* goodness.
eĉ even (adv.).
eduki educate.
edzo married man.
efektiva real, actual.
efektive actually, really.
efiki effect.
eg' denotes increase of degree : *varm'a* warm, *varm'ega* hot.
egala equal.
ej' place where an action occurs ; *kuir'i* to cook, *kuir'ejo* kitchen.
ek' denotes sudden or momentary action ; *krii* cry, *ek'krii* cry out.
eks' ex-, late.
eksciti to excite.
ekster outside, besides.

ĕkstrema extreme.

ekzemplo example.

ekzerci exercise.

ekzisti exist.

ekspozicio exhibition.

el from, out from.

elefanto elephant.

elekti choose.

em' inclined to : *babil'i* chatter, *babil'ema* talkative.

eminenta eminent.

en in ; (when followed by the accusative = into).

enigmo puzzle.

entrepreni undertake.

enui annoy, weary.

envii envy.

epoko epoch.

er' one of many objects of the same kind : *sabl'o* sand, *sabl'ero* grain of sand.

eraro error, mistake.

erinaco hedgehog.

erpi harrow.

esperi hope.

esplori explore.

esprimi express (vb).

esti be.

estimi esteem.

estingi extinguish.

estro chief : *ŝip'o* ship, *ŝip'estro* captain.

et' denotes diminution of degree : *rid'i* laugh, *rid' eti* smile.

etaĝo stage, story (of a house).

eterna eternal.

etiketo etiquette.

eviti avoid.

ezoko pike (fish).

F

fabo bean.

fabelo tale, **story.**

fablo fable.

facila easy.

fadeno thread.

fajfi whistle.

fajli file.

fajro fire.

faksimilo facsimile.

fali fall.

falĉi mow, cut grass.

faldi fold.

falko falcon.

falsa false.

familio family.

fari do, *far'iĝi* become.

faringo throat.

farti be (relating to health).

faruno meal, farina, flour.

fasko bundle.

fasti fast (vb.).

faŭko jaws.

febro fever.

feĉo sediment.

felo hide, fleece.

feliĉa happy.

felto felt.

fenŝi split.
fenestro window.
fero iron.
fermi shut.
festo feast.
fianĉo betrothed (male).
fidela faithful.
fiera proud.
figo fig.
figuro figure, representation.
filo son.
fino end.
fingro finger.
firma firm.
fiŝo fish.
fiska fiscal.
flanko side.
flari smell (vb.).
flati flatter.
flava yellow.
flegi nourish, take care of.
fleksi bend (v. act.).
floro flower.
flui flow.
flugi fly (vb.).
fluida fluid.
fluto flute.
foiro fair (subst.).
fojo time (three " times " etc.).
fojno hay.
foko seal (animal).
folio leaf.
fonto fountain.
for forth, out.
forgesi forget.

forĝi forge.
forko fork.
formiko ant.
forno stove, furnace.
forta strong
fortigi fortify.
fosi dig.
frago strawberry.
fragmento fragment.
frajo spawn
frambo raspberry.
frapi hit.
frato brother.
fraŭlo bachelor.
freneza crazy.
freŝa fresh.
fromaĝo cheese.
frosto frost.
froti rub.
frua early.
frugilego rook.
frukto fruit.
frunto, forehead.
ftizo phthisis, consumption
fulgo soot.
fulmo lightning.
fumi smoke.
fundo, bottom.
funebro, funeral.
fungo mushroom.
futo foot (measure).

G.

gaja gay, merry.
gajni gain.
galo gall.

galoŝo rubber-shoe.
gamaŝo gaiter.
ganto, glove.
garbo sheaf, shock.
gardi guard.
gasto guest.
ge' of both sexes : *patro* father, *ge'patr'o'j* parents.
gento race, kind, genus.
genuo knee.
geranio geranium.
glacio ice.
gladi smoothe, to iron.
glano acorn.
glaso glass, vase.
glata slippery.
glavo sword.
gliti glide, *glit'vetur'ilo* sledge.
globo globe
gloro glory
glui glue.
gluti, swallow (vb.).
golfo, gulf.
gorĝo throat.
grajno a grain.
granda great, tall.
granito, granite.
grasa fat.
grati scratch.
gratuli congratulate.
grava important.
graveda pregnant.
greno grain.
grilo cricket (insect).
grimaco grimace.
griza grey.

groso gooseberry.
gruo crane (bird).
grupo group.
gudro tar.
gumo gum, mucilage.
gusto taste.
guto drop.
gvido guide.

Ĝ.

ĝardeno garden.
ĝemi groan.
ĝeni constrain, embarrass.
ĝentila polite.
ĝi it.
ĝibo hump.
ĝis up to, until.
ĝojo joy.
ĝuste just, exact.

H.

ha ah, alas.
hajlo hail.
haki hew, chop.
halo market, market place.
haladzo exhalation.
halti come to a stop.
haro hair.
haringo herring.
harpo harp.
haŭto skin.
havi have (possess).
hedero ivy.

hejmo home.
hejti heat (vb.).
hela clear, glaring.
helpi help.
hepato liver.
herbo grass.
heredi inherit.
herezo heresy.
hieraŭ yesterday.
himno hymn.
hirudo leech.
hirundo swallow (bird).
ho oh.
hodiaŭ to-day.
hoko hook.
homo man.
honesta honest.
honoro honour.
honto shame.
horo hour.
hordeo barley.
horloĝo clock.
hotelo hotel.
hufo hoof.
humila humble.
humoro humour.
hundo dog.

I.

i termination of the infinitive in verbs: *laŭd'i* to praise.
ia of any kind.
ial for any cause.
iam at any time, ever, once.

id descendant, young one : *bov'o* ox, *bov'ido* calf.
ie anywhere.
iel anyhow.
ies anyone's.
ig' to cause to be : *pur'a* pure, *pur'igi* purify.
iĝ' to become : *ruĝ'a* red, *ruĝ'iĝi* blush.
il' instrument : *tond'i* shear, *tond'ilo* scissors.
ili they.
ilustrajo illustration.
imiti imitate.
in' ending of feminine words : *bov'o* ox, *bov'ino* cow.
inciti provoke, incite.
inda worthy.
industrio industry.
infano child.
infekti infect.
infero hell.
influo influence.
infuzi infuse.
ing' holder for : *kandel'o* candle, *kandel'ingo* candle-stick.
inko ink.
insekto insect.
insisti insist.
instrui instruct, teach.
insulo island.
insulti insult.
int' ending of past part. act. in verbs : *am'inta* having loved.

inteligenta intelligent.
intenci intend.
inter between, among.
interna inner.
intesto intestine.
inviti invite.
io anything.
iom a little.
iri go.
is ending of past tense in verbs: *am'is* loved.
ist' person occupied with: *mar'o* sea, *mar'isto* sailor.
it' ending of past part. pass. in verbs: *am'ita* having been loved.
iu any one.

J.

j sign of the plural: *patr'o* father, *patr'o'j* fathers.
ja indeed.
jako jacket.
jam already.
jaro year.
je (can be rendered by various English prepositions).
jen behold, lo, *jen — jen* sometimes...sometimes.
jes yes.
ju—des the...the.
jubileo jubilee.
jugo yoke.
juĝi judge.

juki itch.
juna young.
jungi couple, harness (vbs.)
jupo petticoat.
justa just, righteous.

Ĵ.

ĵaluza jealous.
ĵaŭdo Thursday.
ĵeti throw.
ĵuri swear.
ĵus just, exactly.

K.

kadro frame.
kafo coffee.
kaĝo cage.
kaj and.
kajero paper covered book, copy-book.
kalo corn (on the foot).
kaldrono kettle.
kaleŝo carriage.
kaliko bowl.
kalko lime.
kalkano heel.
kalkuli calculate.
kalumnii calumniate.
kambio bill of exchange.
kamelo camel.
kameno chimney.
kamomilo chamomile.
kampo field.

kano cane.
kanabo hemp.
kanalo canal.
kanapo sofa, lounge.
vanario canary.
kandelo candle.
kandidato candidate.
kankro crab.
kanti sing.
kapo head.
kapabla capable.
kapro goat.
kapti catch.
kara dear.
karafo caraffe, decanter.
karbo coal.
karesi caress.
karoto carrot.
karpo carp (fish).
kaserolo stewpan.
kasko helmet.
kastelo castle.
kastoro beaver.
kaŝi hide (vb.).
kaŝtano chestnut.
kato cat.
katedro cathedral.
kaŭzi cause.
kavo cave.
kaverno cavern.
ke that (conj.).
kelo cellar.
kelka some.
kelnero waiter.
kerno kernel.
kesto chest, box.
kia what (kind of).

kial why, wherefore.
kiam when.
kie where.
kiel how.
kies whose.
kio what.
kiom how much — how many.
kisi kiss.
kiu who, which (also that = relative).
klafto fathom (measure).
klara clear.
klini bend, incline.
knabo boy.
kojno wedge.
koko rooster.
kolo neck.
kolego colleague, comrade
kolekti collect.
kolera mad, angry.
kolombo dove.
kolono column.
koloro colour.
kolumo collar.
komo comma.
kombi comb.
komedio comedy.
komenci commence.
komerco trade.
komisio commission.
komizo clerk.
komodo chest of drawers.
kompari compare.
kompato compassion.
komplezo favour, liking.
komposti set (type).

kompreni understand.
komuna common.
komuniki communicate.
koncerto concert.
koni know, recognise.
kondičo condition.
konduki condúct.
konduto cónduct.
konfesi confess.
konfidi confide, trust.
konfuzi confuse.
konko shell, mussel.
konkludi conclude.
konscii be conscious of.
konscienco conscience.
konsenti consent.
konservi, preserve.
konsili advise, counsel.
konsoli console.
konstanta, constant.
konstrui construct, build.
kontentigi satisfy.
kontoro bureau, office.
kontraŭ against.
kontroli control.
kontuzo contusion.
konvalo May-lily.
konvena convenient.
konvinki convince.
koro heart.
korbo basket.
kordo string (piano, etc.).
korekti correct.
korespondi correspond.
korko cork.
korno horn.
korpo body.

korto court.
korvo raven.
kosto cost, price.
koto dirt.
kolono cotton.
koturno quail (bird).
koverto envelope.
kovri cover.
kraĉi spit.
krajono pencil.
krampo clamp, holdfast, staple.
kranio cranium.
krano tap, spigot.
kravato cravat.
krei create.
kredi believe.
kremo cream.
kreno horse-radish.
kreski grow, increase.
kreto chalk.
krii cry.
kribro sieve.
krimo crime.
kripla crippled.
kroĉi hook to, cling to.
krono crown.
kruco cross.
kruĉo jug.
kruela cruel.
krusto crust.
kubuto elbow.
kudri sew.
kufo bonnet (woman's).
kuglo bullet.
kuiri cook.
kukolo cuckoo.

kukumo cucumber.
kulo gnat.
kulero spoon.
kulpo fault, blame.
kun with, *kun'e* together.
kuniklo rabbit.
kupro copper.
kuri run.
kuraci cure, heal (v. a.).
kuraĝo courage.
kurba curved.
kurso course (lessons).
kurteno curtain.
kuseno cushion.
kuŝi lie (down).
kutimo custom.
kuzo cousin.
kvankam although.
kvar four.
kvazaŭ as if.
kverko oak.
kvieta calm, quiet.
kvin five.

L.

l'
la } the.
laboro labour.
laca weary.
lacerto lizard.
lado tinned iron.
lago lake.
lakto milk.
lama lame.
lampo lamp.

lano wool.
lando land, country.
lango tongue.
lanterno lantern.
lanugo down, fluff.
lardo lard.
larĝa broad.
larmo tear (to shed a).
lasi leave, let alone.
lasta last, latest.
laŭ according to.
laŭbo arbour, summer-house.
laŭdi praise.
laŭta loud.
lavango avalanche.
lavi wash.
leciono lesson.
ledo leather.
legendo legend.
legi read.
legomo legume.
leĝo law.
leki lick.
lento lentil.
leono lion.
leporo hare.
lerni learn.
lerta skilful.
letero letter.
levi lift, raise.
li he.
libera free.
libro book, *libr'o'ten'ad'o* book-keeping.
lieno spleen.
ligi bind, tie.

ligno wood (the substance).
likvoro liqueur.
limo limit.
limako snail.
lino flax.
lingvo language.
lipo lip.
lito bed.
litero letter (of the alphabet).
logi entice.
loĝi lodge, dwell.
loko place.
longa long.
loterio lottery.
loti cast lots.
lui rent.
ludi play.
luma light, *mal'luma* dark.
luno moon.
lundo Monday.
lupo wolf.
lupolo hops.
luto solder.

M.

maco unleavened bread.
maĉi chew.
magazeno store.
maizo maize.
majesto majesty.
majstro master.
makleristo broker.
makulo stain.
mal' denotes opposites.

maleolo ankle.
malgraŭ in spite of.
mano hand.
manĝi eat.
maniero manner.
maniko sleeve.
mantelo cloak, mantle.
maro sea.
marĉo swamp, marsh.
marĉandi bargain, haggle.
mardo Tuesday.
marĝeno margin.
marmoro marble.
martelo hammer.
masoni build with stone,
  mason'isto mason.
masto mast.
mastro master.
maŝo mesh.
maŝino machine.
mateno morning.
matraco mattress.
matura ripe.
meblo piece of furniture.
meĉo wick.
medaliono medallion.
mejlo mile.
melo badger.
meleagro turkey.
melki milk (vb.)
melodramo melodrama.
melono melon.
mem self, same.
membro member.
memoro memory.
mensogi tell a lie.
mentono chin.

meriti merit.

merkredo Wednesday.

meti put, place.

metio handicraft.

mevo sea-gull.

mezo middle.

mezuri measure.

mi I.

mielo honey.

migdalo almond.

migri migrate, *en'migr'-ant'o* immigrant.

miksi mix.

mil thousand.

milio millet.

militi fight.

minaci menace, threat.

miopo short-sight.

miozoto forget-me-not.

miri wonder.

mirto myrtle.

mistero mystery.

mizero distress, misery.

modelo model.

modera moderate.

modesta modest.

moduli modulate.

mola soft.

mono money (coin).

monato month.

mondo world.

monto mountain.

montri show.

monumento monument.

moro habit, usage.

mordi bite.

mergaŭ to-morrow.

morti die.

mošto universal title : *Vi'a reĝ'a mošt'o* your majesty, *vi'a mošt'o* your honour.

movi move (v. n.).

mueli mill.

multa much, many.

muro wall.

murmuri murmur.

muso mouse.

musko moss.

mustardo mustard.

mušo fly (a).

muta dumb.

muzeo museum.

muziko music.

N.

n ending of the objective, also marks direction.

nacio nation.

naĝi swim.

najbaro neighbour.

najlo nail.

najtingalo nightingale.

naski bear, produce, *nask'iĝi* be born.

naturo nature.

naŭ nine.

nazo nose.

naztuko pocket handkerchief.

ne no, not.

nebulo fog.

necesa necessary.

neĝo snow.

nek—nek neither—nor.

nenia no kind of.

neniam never.

nenie nowhere.

neniel nohow.

nenies no one's.

nenio nothing.

neniu nobody.

nepo grandson.

nerva nervous.

nesto nest.

nevo nephew.

ni we.

nigra black.

nj' diminutive of female names.

nobelo nobleman.

nobla noble.

nokto night.

nomo name.

nombro number.

nordo north.

noti note.

nova new.

nu well!

nubo cloud.

nuda naked.

nuko nape of the neck.

nukso nut.

nulo zero.

numero number (of a magazine, etc.).

nun now.

nur only (adv.).

nutri nourish.

O.

o ending of nouns (subst.), root *patr'* : *patr'o* father.

obei obey.

objekto object.

obl' ...-fold, *du* two, *du'obla* twofold, duplex.

obstina obstinate.

oceano ocean.

odoro odour.

ofendi offend.

oferi offer (sacrifice).

ofico office.

ofte often.

ok eight.

okazi happen, *okaz'o* occasion.

okcidento west.

oktavo octave (mus.).

okulo eye, *okulvitroj* spectacles.

okupi occupy.

ol than.

oleo oil.

ombro shadow.

ombrelo umbrella.

ono marks fractions : *kvar* four, *kvar'ono* a fourth, quarter.

ondo wave.

oni one, people, they : *oni dir'as* they say, it is said.

onklo uncle.

onta ending of fut. part. act. in verbs : *am'onta* about to love.

op' marks collective nume-
rals : *tri* three, *tri'op'e*
three together.

opalo opal.

oportuna opportune, suitable.

oro gold.

oranĝo orange.

ordo order, regularity.

ordinara ordinary.

ordoni order, command.

orelo ear.

orfo orphan.

orgeno organ (musical).

oriento east.

ornami ornament.

os ending of future tense
in verbs: *am'os* will love.

oscedi yawn.

osto bone.

ostro oyster.

ota ending of fut. part.
pass. in verbs : *am'ota*
about to be loved.

ovo egg.

P.

paco peace.

pacienco patience.

pafi shoot.

pagi pay.

paĝo page (of a book).

pagodo pagoda.

pajlo straw.

paki pack, put up.

pala pale.

palaco palace.

palato palate.

palpi touch, feel.

palpebro eyelid.

pamfleto pamphlet.

pano bread.

pantalono pants, trousers.

pantoflo slipper.

papago parrot.

papavo poppy.

papero paper.

papilio butterfly.

paradizo paradise.

pardoni forgive.

parenco relation.

parko park.

paroli speak.

parto part.

pasi pass.

pasamento lace.

pasero sparrow.

pasio passion.

pasko Easter.

pasto paste.

pastro priest, pastor.

paŝo stride, step.

paŝti pasture, feed animals.

pato frying-pan.

patro father, *patr'ujo* father
land.

patrioto patriot.

pavo peacock.

pavimo pavement.

peco piece.

pego woodpecker.

peko sin.

peli pursue, chase out.
pelto fur.
peni endeavour, to try to.
pendi hang.
peniko paintbrush.
penco penny.
pensi think.
pentri paint.
per through, by means of.
perĉo perch (fish).
perdi lose.
perdriko partridge,
perei perish.
perfekta perfect.
perfidi betray.
perlo pearl.
perlamoto mother-of-pearl.
permesi permit, allow.
perono front-steps.
persekuti persecute.
persiko peach.
persono person.
pesi weigh (vb. act.).
pesto plague.
peti request, beg.
petola petulant.
petrolo coal-oil, kerosene.
petroselo parsley.
pezi weigh (vb. neut.).
pia pious.
piedo foot.
pigo magpie.
piki prick, sting.
pilko ball (to play with).
pino pine-tree.
pinĉi pinch.
pinglo pin.

pipo pipe (tobacco).
pipro pepper.
piro pear.
piramido pyramid.
pizo pea.
placo public square.
plaĉi please.
plado plate.
plafono ceiling.
plando sole (of the foot).
planko floor.
planti plant (vb.).
plata flat, plain.
plej most.
plekti weave, plait.
plena full.
plendi complain.
plezuro pleasure.
pli more.
plori mourn, weep.
plugi to plough.
plumo pen.
plumbo lead (metal).
pluvi rain.
po by (with numbers) : *po
  kvar* at the rate of four
poemo poem.   [each.
poeto poet.
polico police.
poligono buckwheat.
polvo dust.
pomo apple.
ponto bridge.
poplo poplar.
popolo people.
por for.
porcelano porcelain.

pordo door.
porko hog.
porti carry.
portreto portrait.
posedi possess.
post after, behind.
postuli require, claim.
poŝo pocket.
poŝt' post, *sign'o de poŝt'o* postage-stamp, *poŝt'o'kart'o* postal-card.
poto pot.
povi be able, can.
prava right (to be in the right).
precipe particularly.
preciza precise.
prediki preach.
preĝi pray.
premi press.
preni take.
prepari prepare.
presi print (vb.).
preskaŭ almost.
preta ready.
preter beside, beyond.
prezidanto president.
prezenti present (vb.).
prezo prize.
pri concerning, about.
princo prince.
printempo spring time, the spring.
privata private.
pro for the sake of.
procento per cent.
procesio procession.

profunda deep.
proksima near.
promeni to walk, promenade.
promesi promise.
proponi propose, suggest.
propra own (one's own).
prosperi prosper.
provo attempt, trial.
proverbo proverb.
provinco province.
prudenta prudent.
pruno plum.
prunto loan, *doni prunte* to lend, *peti prunte* to borrow.
pruvi prove, demonstrate.
pugno fist.
pulmo lung.
pulvo gunpowder.
pulvoro powder.
pumpi pump.
puni punish.
punkto point.
pupo doll.
pura pure.
puritano puritan.
puso pus, matter.
puŝi push.
puto well (subst.).
putra rotten.

R.

rabi rob.
rabato rebate, discount.
rabeno rabbin.

raboti plane.
rado wheel.
radio beam, ray.
radiko root.
rafano radish.
rajto right, authority.
rakonti tell, relate.
rampi crawl.
rano frog.
rando edge.
rapo turnip.
rapida quick, rapid.
raso breed, race.
rato rat.
raŭka hoarse.
raŭpo caterpillar.
ravi ravish, enrapture.
razi shave.
re' again, back.
refuti refute.
regi rule, reign.
regali entertain, regale.
regimento regiment.
regno kingdom.
regulo rule.
reĝo king.
rekompenci reward.
rekta straight, *mal'rekta* oblique, sloping.
religio religion.
relo rail.
remi row (vb.).
reno kidney.
renkonti meet.
renversi upset.
respondi reply.
resti remain.

reto net.
revo fancy.
ribo currant.
ribelo, rebel, insurgent.
ricevi obtain, get, receive.
riĉa rich.
ridi laugh.
rigardi behold, look at.
rigli to bolt or bar.
rikolti reap.
rilati be related to.
rimo rhyme.
rimarki remark.
rimedo, means, remedy.
rimeno strap.
ringo ring (subst.).
ripo, rib.
ripeti repeat.
ripozi, repose.
riproĉi reproach.
rivero river.
rizo rice.
romanco, romance.
rompi break.
ronda round.
roso dew.
rosti roast.
rozo rose.
rubando ribbon.
ruĝa red.
ruli roll.
rumo rum.
rusto rust.
ruza trick, ruse.

S.

sabato Saturday.
sablo sand.
safiro sapphire.
sago arrow.
saĝa wise.
sagaca, sagacious.
sako sack.
salo salt.
salajro wages, salary.
saliko willow.
salmo salmon.
salti leap, jump.
saluti salute, greet.
sama same.
sana healthy.
sango blood.
sankta holy.
sapo soap
sata satisfied, satiated, mal'sata hungry.
saŭco sauce.
savi save
sceno scene (theatre).
scii know.
scienco science
sciuro squirrel.
se if.
sebo tallow.
sed but.
segi saw.
seĝo seat, chair.
seka dry.
sekalo rye.
sekreto secret.
sekvi follow.

selo saddle.
semi sow.
semajno week.
sen without.
senco sense.
sendi send.
senti feel, perceive.
sep seven.
serĉi search.
serpento serpent.
seruro lock (subst.).
servi serve.
ses six.
severa severe.
sezono season.
si one's self.
sidi sit.
sigeli seal (vb).
signo sign, token
signifi signify, mean.
silabo syllable, silab'i to spell.
silenta silent.
siliko flint.
silko silk.
simio monkey.
simila like, similar.
simpla simple.
sinjoro Sir, Mr.
sitelo bucket.
situacio situation.
skandali scandalise.
skarabo beetle.
skatolo small box, case.
skribi write.
skui shake.
skulpti sculpture.

skvamo scale (fish, etc.).
sobra sober.
societo society.
soifo thirst.
sojlo threshold.
sola only, alone.
soldato soldier.
solena solemn.
solvi loosen, dissolve.
somero summer.
sonĝi dream.
sono sound (subst.).
sonori give out a sound (as a bell, etc.).
soprano soprano.
sorĉo witchcraft.
sorto fate, lot.
sovaĝa wild, savage.
speco kind, species.
spegulo looking-glass.
sperto experience.
spezi spend, *el'spez'o'j* expenses.
spico spice.
spiko ear, head (of corn, etc.).
spinaco spinach.
spiri breathe.
spirito spirit.
spongo sponge.
sprito wit.
sprono spur.
stacio depôt (railroad).
stalo stable.
stampo stamp, mark.
stano tin.
standardo flag.

stango pole.
stari stand.
stato state, condition.
stelo star.
stomako stomach.
stranga strange.
strato street.
streko streak, line.
strigo owl.
struto ostrich.
studento student.
sturno starling.
sub under, beneath, below.
subita sudden.
substanco substance.
suĉi suck.
sudo south.
suferi suffer.
sufiĉa sufficient.
sufoki suffocate.
suko sap, juice.
sukceno amber.
sukceso success.
sukero sugar.
sulfuro sulphur.
sultano sultan.
suno sun.
supo soup.
super over, above.
supozi suppose.
supra upper (adj.).
sur upon, on.
surda deaf.
surtuto coat.
suspekti suspect.

Ŝ.

ŝafo sheep.
ŝajni seem.
ŝako(j) chess.
ŝanceli totter.
ŝanĝi change.
ŝargi load (a gun, etc.).
ŝaŭmo foam.
ŝelo shell.
ŝerco joke.
ŝi she.
ŝildo shield.
ŝilingo shilling.
ŝinko bacon, ham.
ŝipo ship.
ŝiri tear, rend.
ŝlimo slime.
ŝlosi lock, fasten.
ŝmiri smear.
ŝnuro string.
ŝoveli shovel.
ŝpari be sparing, *ŝpar'em'ec'o* thrift.
ŝpini spin.
ŝpruci sprinkle.
ŝranko cupboard.
ŝraŭbo screw.
ŝtalo steel.
ŝtato state, *Unu'ig'it'a'j Ŝtat'o'j* United States.
ŝteli steal.
ŝtofo stuff, matter, goods.
ŝtono stone.
ŝtopi stop, fasten down.
ŝtrumpo stocking.
ŝtupo step.
ŝuo shoe.
ŝuldi owe.
ŝultro shoulder.
ŝuti discharge (corn etc.)
ŝveli swell.
ŝviti perspire.

T.

tabako tobacco.
tablo table.
tabulo tablet.
tago day.
tajloro tailor.
takso tax.
talpo mole (animal).
tamburo drum.
tamen however, neverthe-less.
tapeto tapestry.
tapiŝo carpet.
taso cup.
taŭgi be fit for, *taŭg'a* serviceable.
teo tea.
teda tedious.
tegmento roof.
teksi weave.
tempo time.
tempio temple (of fore-head).
teni hold, grasp.
tenti tempt.
tero earth.
teritorio territory.

terni sneeze.
teruro terror.
testudo tortoise.
tetro (*c.f. urogalo*) grouse.
tia such.
tial therefore.
tiam then.
tie there.
tiel thus, so.
tikli tickle.
timi fear.
tineo moth.
tio that one.
tiom so much.
tiri draw, pull, drag.
tiu that.
tolo linen.
toleri tolerate.
tombo tomb, grave.
tondi clip, shear
tondro thunder.
topazo topaz.
tordi wind, twist.
torni turn (on a lathe).
tornistro knapsack.
tra through
trabo beam (of wood).
traduki translate.
trafi strike, meet, fall in with.
trakti transact.
tranĉi cut.
rankvila quiet.
trans across.
tre very.
tremi tremble.
trempi immerse.

treni drag, trail.
tri three.
triangulo triangle.
trinki drink.
tritiko wheat.
tro too (much).
trompi deceive, cheat.
trono throne.
trotuaro side-walk.
trovi find.
truo hole.
trumpeto trumpet.
trunko trunk, stem
tualeto, toilette.
tubo tube.
tubero bulb.
tuj immediately
tuko cloth.
tulipo tulip.
turo tower.
turdo thrush.
turkiso turquoise.
turmenti torment.
turni turn (vb.).
tusi cough.
tuŝi touch.
tuta whole.

U.

u' ending of the imperative in verbs.
uj' containing, bearing : *ink'o* ink, *ink'ujo* ink-pot ; *pom'o* apple, *pom'ujo* apple - tree ; *Turk'ujo* Turkey.

ul' person noted for . . . :
  avar'a covetous, *avar'ul'o* miser, covetous person.
ulcero ulcer.
um' this syllable has no fixed meaning, *plen'a* full, *plen'vmi* fulfil ; *am'inda* worthy of love, *am'ind'umi* make love.
ungo nail (finger).
uniformo uniform (costume).
universala universal.
unu one.
urbo town.
urogalo grouse.
urso bear (animal).
urtiko nettle.
us ending of conditional in verbs.
utila useful.
uzi use.
uzurpi usurp.

V.

vakso **wax.**
valo valley.
valizo valise.
vana vain, needless.
vango cheek.
vaporo steam, vapour.
variolo smallpox.
varma warm.
vasta wide, vast.
vato padding, wadding.
vazo **vase.**

vejno vein.
veki wake, arouse.
velo sail (subst.).
velki fade.
veluro velvet.
veni come.
vendi sell.
vendredo Friday.
veneno poison.
vengo vengeance.
venki conquer.
vento wind.
ventro belly.
vera true.
verbo verb.
verda green.
verko work (literary).
vermo worm.
verso verse.
verŝi pour.
veruko wart.
vespo wasp.
vespero evening.
vesperto bat.
vesti clothe, *vest'o* clothes.
veŝto vest.
veti bet, wager.
vetero weather.
veturi journey, travel.
veziko blister, bladder.
viando meat, flesh.
vico row, rank.
vidi see.
vidvo widower.
vigla brisk, alert.
vikaro vicar.
vilaĝo village.

vino wine, *vin'bero* grape, *sek'vin'bero* raisin.

vinagro vinegar.

vintro winter.

violo violet.

violkolora violet (colour).

violono violin.

vipo whip.

viro man.

virto virtue.

viŝi wipe.

vitro glass (substance).

vivi live.

vizaĝo face.

voĉo voice.

vojo way, road.

vojaĝo voyage.

voki call.

voli wish, will.

volonte willingly.

volumo volume.

volvi turn round, roll up.

vorto word.

vosto tail.

vulpo fox.

vulturo vulture.

vundi wound.

Z.

zenito zenith.

zinko zinc.

zigzaga zigzag.

zono girdle, belt.

zorgo care for.

NOTE ON THE USE OF THE ACCUSATIVE (N).

N, the accusative termination, is not only used to mark the direct object of a verb, as already shown; it is also used as follows:—

1. To denote motion towards, whenever the preposition does not clearly do so. La hundo kuris en la ĝardenon. The dog ran *into* the garden. Kien li iras? Where is he going? Li prenos la aferon sur sin, ne timu. He will take the matter upon himself, don't fear.

2. To denote the duration of an event. Li restis tri tagojn en Romo. He stayed three days in Rome. Mi dormos ses horojn. I shall sleep (during) six hours.

3. To denote dates, etc. Li alvenos lundon. He will arrive on Monday. Mi skribis al li la dekan (tagon) de Junio. I wrote to him on the tenth of June. La 27an Aŭgusto, 1904a. Mi vin vidis sabaton. I saw you on Saturday.

4. To denote price, weight, and measure. Tiu ĉi libro kostas tri ŝilingojn. This book costs three shillings. Mia domo estas alta 53 futojn. My house is 53 feet high (in height).

APPENDIX.

NAMES OF COUNTRIES, Etc.

Afriko,	Africa.	*Ĥinujo,*	China.
Ameriko,	America.	*Italujo,*	Italy.
Aŭstralio,	Australia.	*Irlando,*	Ireland.
Azio,	Asia.	*Japanujo,*	Japan.
Eŭropo,	Europe.	*Meksiko,*	Mexico.
Alĝerio,	Algiers.	*Norda Ameriko,* }	N. America.
Anglujo, Anglolando, }	England.	*Norvegujo,*	Norway.
Belgujo,	Belgium.	*Palestino,*	Palestine.
Brazilujo,	Brazil.	*Persujo,*	Persia.
Danujo,	Denmark.	*Portugalujo,*	Portugal.
Egiptujo,	Egypt.	*Prusujo.*	Prussia.
Finnlando,	Finland.	*Rumanujo,*	Roumania.
Francujo, Francolando, }	France.	*Rusujo,*	Russia.
		Skotlando,	Scotland.
Germanujo,	Germany.	*Serbujo,*	Servia.
Granda Britujo, }	Gt. Britain.	*Suda Ameriko,*	S. America.
		Svedujo,	Sweden.
Grekujo,	Greece.	*Svisujo,*	Switzerland
Hispanujo,	Spain.	*Turkujo,*	Turkey.
Holando,	Holland.	*Unuigitaj Ŝtatoj Amerikaj,* }	United States of America.
Hungarujo,	Hungary.		

NAMES OF CITIES.

Amsterdamo,	Amsterdam.	*Parizo,*	Paris.
Berlino,	Berlin.	*Pekino,*	Pekin.
Edinburgo,	Edinburgh.	*Prago,*	Prague.
Lisabono,	Lisbon.	*Romo,*	Rome.
Londono,	London.	*Sankt Peter-*	St. Peters-
Madrido,	Madrid.	*burgo,*	burg.
Moskvo,	Moscow.	*Tuniso,*	Tunis.
Neapolo,	Naples.	*Varsovio,*	Warsaw.
Nov-Jorko,	New York.	*Vieno,*	Vienna.
Odeso,	Odessa.		

NAMES OF PEOPLES.

Anglo,	Englishman.	*Eŭropano,*	European.
Arabo,	Arab.	*Amerikano,*	American.
Belgo,	Belgian.	*Afrikano,*	African.
Dano,	Dane.	*Aziano,*	Asiatic.
Franco,	Frenchman.	*Irlandano,*	Irishman.
Germano,	German.	*Skotlandano,*	Scotchman.
Greko,	Greek.	*Egipto,*	Egyptian.
Hispano,	Spaniard.	*Zuluo,*	Zulu.
Hungaro,	Hungarian	*Kanadano,*	Canadian.
Londonano,	Londoner.	*Nov-Jorkano,*	New Yorker.

NAMES OF THE MONTHS.

Januaro,	January.	*Julio,*	July.
Februaro,	February.	*Aŭgusto,*	August.
Marto,	March.	*Septembro,*	September.
Aprilo,	April.	*Oktobro,*	October.
Majo,	May.	*Novembro,*	November.
Junio,	June.	*Decembro.*	December.

DAYS OF THE WEEK, Etc.

Lundo,	Monday.	*Horo,*	Hour.
Mardo,	Tuesday.	*Minuto,*	Minute.
Merkredo,	Wednesday.	*Sekundo,*	Second.
Ĵaŭdo,	Thursday.	*Hodiaŭ,*	To-day.
Vendredo,	Friday.	*Morgaŭ,*	To-morrow.
Sabato,	Saturday.	*Hieraŭ,*	Yesterday.
Dimanĉo,	Sunday.	*Mateno,*	Morning.
Jaro,	Year.	*Vespero,*	Evening.
Superjaro,	Leap year.	*Nokto,*	Night.
Monato,	Month.	*Tagmezo,*	Mid-day.
Semajno,	Week.	*Noktomezo,*	Midnight.
Tago,	Day.		

THE SEASONS.

Sezono, Season.　*Printempo,* Spring.　*Somero,* Summer.
Aŭtuno, Autumn.　*Vintro,* Winter.

ARTICLES OF FOOD.

Kafo,	Coffee.	*Ovo,*	Egg.
Teo,	Tea.	*Butero,*	Butter.
Ĉokolado,	Chocolate.	*Mielo,*	Honey.
Akvo,	Water.	*Sukero,*	Sugar.
Vino,	Wine.	*Fromaĝo,*	Cheese.
Biero,	Beer.	*Pano,*	Bread.
Brando,	Brandy.	*Faruno,*	Flour.
Lakto,	Milk.	*Frukto,*	Fruit.
Kremo,	Cream.	*Supo,*	Soup.
Pipro,	Pepper.	*Vermiĉelo,*	Vermicelli.
Salo,	Salt.	*Makarono,*	Macaroni.
Mustardo,	Mustard.	*Supo testuda,*	Turtle soup.

Supo fazeola, Haricot soup. *Pureo,* Purée.

Buljono, { Beef tea (bouillon). *Pizetoj,* Green peas.
Rafano, Radish.

Terpomo, Potato. *Manĝajetoj,* Hors d'œuvre.
Salmo, Salmon. *Reno,* Kidney.
Truto, Trout. *Fiŝo,* Fish.
Haringo, Herring. *Saŭco,* Sauce.
Karpo, Carp. *Vinagro,* Vinegar.
Ostroj, Oysters. *Viandoj*
Legomoj, Vegetables. *Malvarmaj.* } Cold meats.

Ansero kun kaŝtanoj, Goose with chestnuts.
Anaso kun olivoj, Duck with olives.
Kokido rostita, Roast chicken.
Renoj de ŝafido, Mutton kidneys.
Flora-brasiko, Cauliflower.
Asparagoj kun blanka saŭco, Asparagus with white sauce.

Spinaco kun viandsuko, Spinach with gravy.
Terpomoj frititaj, Fried potatoes.
Rostita aŭ bolita bovaĵo, Roasted or boiled beef.
Bifsteko, rosbifo, Beefsteak, roast beef.
Kotletoj de ŝafido, de bovido, Lamb cutlets, veal cutlets.
Ŝinko el Jorko, York ham.
Latuko, Lettuce, etc.

EMINENT MEN ON ESPERANTO.

COUNT TOLSTOY.

When, a few years ago, some persons acquainted with Esperanto wrote to Count Leo Tolstoy, the celebrated author and philosopher, to ask an expression of his opinion on the subject of a universal language, Tolstoy replied as follows :—

Gentlemen,—There cannot exist the slightest doubt that mankind tends ever to form but one family, having for sole guides wisdom and love, and that one of the best means of attaining to this ideal is to arrive at a mutual comprehension. But, in order that the peoples may comprehend one another, it is necessary either that all the languages should reduce themselves to a single one, which can happen but after a very long time—if indeed ever. Or, that a knowledge of all languages shall become so general that not only shall works be translated into every one of these tongues, but everyone shall understand them all so well as to be able to make himself intelligible to all mankind, by the aid now of this one, now of that. Or, better still, that all shall choose a language the study of which shall be obligatory to each people. Or, finally, as the partisans of Volapük and Esperanto suppose, that all men of all nations shall adopt and understand an international language, artificial and simple. This last hypothesis appears to me most reasonable, the most serious, the most easy to be realized.

Such is my reply to the first point. As regards the second—to what extent Esperanto satisfies the requirements of an international language—I cannot reply in a manner altogether decisive, not being a competent judge of this question. I know one thing, however, and that is that I have found Volapük extremely complicated, and Esperanto, on the other hand, very simple—as indeed every European must find it. It is so easy to understand that, when I· received, some six years since, a grammar, a dictionary and some articles in this language, I was able, in two short hours, if not to write, at any rate to read, the language fluently.

In any event, the sacrifices any speaker of a European tongue would make, in devoting some time to the study of Esperanto, are so small and the results which could thereby be achieved so enormous, if all, at least Europeans and Americans—all Christendom—should comprehend this tongue, that the attempt, at least, should be made.

I have often thought that there is no more Christian science than the study of languages, that study which permits of our communicating and allying ourselves with an incalculable number of our fellow men, and I have often remarked how people bear themselves as enemies to one another, solely because they have no means of intercommunication. The study of Esperanto, then, and its diffusion, is assuredly a Christian labour, which hastens the coming of the kingdom of God, the main—I should say, the only—aim of human life

Leo Tolstoy.

Max Müller.

When the staff of a well-known Russian literary association addressed a request to the master-linguist of the age, Max Müller, for his opinion on the various projects of universal language that have appeared during the last few years, the answer received was this :

Dear Sir,—I have frequently had to express my opinion as to the merits of the various schemes of a Universal Language. Each one of these seems to possess some special advantages and disadvantages, but I should certainly place the Esperanto system very high amongst its rivals.

Yours faithfully,

F. Max Müller.

ĈU LA VIRINO MALSUPERAS LA VIRON.

(By Max O'Rell).

Antaŭ multe da jaroj, komitato kunsidis por diskuti
ĉu la virino posedas animon. Mi forgesas kiun
konkludon la kunsido saĝa prenis, sed estas certe ke
la plej parto de viroj kredas ke la virino posedas
animon, kvankam granda nombro de ili ankoraŭ
opinias ke la virino estas kreitaĵo pli malbona
ol la viro. Ili opinias ke la viro estas la majstra
laboraĵo, la lasta vorto de la Tutpotenculo. Sed,
ĉu, tio-ĉi estas vere la okazo? Unue Dio kreis
la teron, due la lumon, post tio Li kreis la fiŝojn, la
birdojn kaj la diversajn bestojn. Poste, Li diris
"Mi nun volas krei estaĵon plej bonan ol la aliaj
bestoj." Li prenis ŝlimon, notu bone, mi diras ŝlimon,
kaj kreis Adamon. En Lia saĝeco Li opiniis ke
ŝlimo ne estis sufiĉe bona por krei la virinon, kaj por
ŝin krei Li prenis materialon jam purigitan per Lia
spiro Dia, Li prenis parton de Adamo kaj kreis per ĝi
Evon. Certe, miaj karaj samhomoj, vi devas
konfesi, aŭ ke la ŝlimo estas pli bona materialo ol vi
mem aŭ ke la virino havas pli noblan devenon ol vi.
Vi ne povas alie klarigi la aferon. Mi vin petas observi
la vicon de la kreadon ; fiŝoj, birdoj, bestoj, la viro,
la virino. Se la viro ne volas konfesi ke la Kreinto
komencis per la plej malbonaj kreitaĵoj kaj finis per
la plej bonaj, li devas konkludi ke la angiloj,
krokodiloj, ŝarkoj, strigoj, agloj kaj paseroj lin
superas.

Se la viro ne volas konfesi la superecon de tiuj-ĉi bestoj super li, li devas konkludi ke la kreadon pliboniĝas ĉiun tagon. Sed la viro diras ke la virino ne estas tiel forta kiel li. Certe ne! Sed la ĉevalo estas pli forta ol la homo, la elefanto trotante sur li pulvorigus lin. La cervo estas pli rapida ol la homo. La kamelo portas sur sia dorso pezon de 2,500 funtoj. La birdoj flugas kaj la homo nur provas flugmaŝinojn. Ĉu la viro estas pli inteligenta ol la virino? Certe ne. Kiu manĝis la pomon? Mi scias ke Evo malobeis antaŭ ol Adamo, sed ŝi havis *ideon* tamen kaj antaŭ ol Adamo. Ĉu li eĉ havis la potencon por kontraŭstari? Ne. Ĉu li eĉ penis defendi la virinon post la ofendado? Ne, li ne ŝin defendis, la timemulo. Li sin turnis kontraŭ ŝin, ŝin riproĉante esti la kaŭzo de la tuta peko. Malbona komenco, malgaja okazo kiun la viro uzis, kaj ĝis hodiaŭ li turnis sin kontraŭ la virinon kiun li trompis kaj ofte ŝin forlasis. La viro estas ankoraŭ fidela al sia deveno. Sinjoroj, la pruvo ke Dio estis kontenta kreinte la virinon kaj dirinte Sian lastan vorton pri Sia laboro Dia estas ke Li konfidis al ŝi la plej noolan mision, naski la estontajn generaciojn, porti la infanojn al la mondo, konduki iliajn unuajn paŝojn, disvolvi iliajn animojn kaj veki en ili la amon al tio kio estas bona kaj ĝusta. Dedicinte al la virino la patrinecon, Dio proklamis la superecon de la virino super la ceteraj kreitaĵoj.

From the " Courrier International."

(Done into Esperanto by Madame Louise Lombard).

The Standard Series
ESPERANTO

Esperanto
Student's Complete Text Book. Cloth, boards, 50c. net.

English-Esperanto Dictionary
By J. C. O'Connor and C. F. HAYES. Boards, 60c. net.

Esperanto-English Dictionary
By A. MOTTEAU. Boards, 60c. net.

Esperanto Primer
Containing Grammar, Vocabulary and Exercises, with Key, by J. C. O'CONNOR, PH.D. Paper, 10c. net..

Handy Pocket Vocabulary
English-Esperanto and Esperanto-English, by J. C. O'CONNOR, B.A. Paper, 10c. net.

A First Reader in Esperanto
By E. A. LAWRENCE. Cloth, 25c. net.

Lessons in Esperanto
Based on DR. ZAMENHOF'S "EKZERCARO." By GEORGE W. BULLEN. Cloth, 25c. net.

Dickens' Christmas Carol
Paper, 40c. net; cloth, 60c. net.

CPSIA information can be obtained
at www.ICGtesting.com
Printed in the USA
LVOW04s1539101215

466281LV00018B/1200/P